PRAYING FOR TEEN GIRLS

Also by Stacey Thacker

Being OK with Where You Are

Fresh Out of Amazing

Hope for the Weary Mom
(cowritten with Brooke McGlothlin)

Hope for the Weary Mom Devotional: A 40-Day Journey
(cowritten with Brooke McGlothlin)

Is Jesus Worth It?

Threadbare Prayer

Unraveled: Hope for the Mom at the End of Her Rope
(cowritten with Brooke McGlothlin)

When Grace Walks In

PRAYING FOR
TEEN
GIRLS

PARTNER WITH GOD FOR THE HEART OF YOUR DAUGHTER

STACEY THACKER

BETHANYHOUSE

a division of Baker Publishing Group
Minneapolis, Minnesota

© 2025 by Stacey Thacker

Published by Bethany House Publishers
Minneapolis, Minnesota
BethanyHouse.com

Bethany House Publishers is a division of
Baker Publishing Group, Grand Rapids, Michigan

Printed in the United States of America

Library of Congress Cataloging-in-Publication Data
Names: Thacker, Stacey, author.
Title: Praying for teen girls : partner with God for the heart of your daughter / Stacey Thacker.
Description: Minneapolis, Minnesota : Bethany House Publishers, a division of Baker Publishing Group, [2025] | Includes bibliographical references.
Identifiers: LCCN 2024017701 | ISBN 9780764243738 (paperback) | ISBN 9780764244650 (casebound) | ISBN 9781493449699 (ebook)
Subjects: LCSH: Teenage girls—Prayers and devotions. | Teenage girls—Religious life. | Christian teenagers—Religious life. | Prayer—Christianity.
Classification: LCC BV4860 .T43 2025 | DDC 248.8/431—dc23/eng/20240613
LC record available at https://lccn.loc.gov/2024017701

Unless otherwise indicated, Scripture quotations are from THE HOLY BIBLE, NEW INTERNATIONAL VERSION®, NIV® Copyright © 1973, 1978, 1984, 2011 by Biblica, Inc.® Used by permission. All rights reserved worldwide.

Scripture quotations labeled ESV are from The Holy Bible, English Standard Version® (ESV®), copyright © 2001 by Crossway, a publishing ministry of Good News Publishers. Used by permission. All rights reserved. ESV Text Edition: 2016

Scripture quotations labeled MSG are taken from THE MESSAGE, copyright © 1993, 2002, 2018 by Eugene H. Peterson. Used by permission of NavPress. All rights reserved. Represented by Tyndale House Publishers, Inc.

Scripture quotations labeled NLT are from the Holy Bible, New Living Translation, copyright © 1996, 2004, 2015 by Tyndale House Foundation. Used by permission of Tyndale House Publishers, Carol Stream, Illinois 60188. All rights reserved.

Cover design by Micah Kandros Design

Published in association with Books & Such Literary Management, www.booksandsuch.com.

Baker Publishing Group publications use paper produced from sustainable forestry practices and postconsumer waste whenever possible.

25 26 27 28 29 30 31   7 6 5 4 3 2 1

For Emma, Abigail, Caroline, and Alison

"Because he bends down to listen,
I will pray [for you] as long as I have breath."
Psalm 116:2 NLT

CONTENTS

FOREWORD

When I was raising my daughter, my goal was to raise her into the woman of God that He had called her to be and to help her find her purpose. At first, as a rather new Christian, I had no idea where to begin. But as my walk matured and my faith grew, I realized that prayer was the best place to start.

I wasn't sure how to pray for my daughter during her teenage years, but I knew it was critical that I did pray. And my prayers were answered—some exactly how I had hoped and others not how I had hoped at all, but ultimately the best answers because they were His answers.

Whether we like it or not, motherhood is a journey of letting go. Our children do go, and there is nothing we could (or should) do to stop them. What can we do as we grow them to go? We can pray, and we can model what a life of prayer looks like in the good times and the not-so-good times we will all face.

When my daughter's teenage years arrived, Facebook, Instagram, Twitter, and TikTok didn't exist. In fact, there was no social media at all. Honestly, that made it a lot easier to parent, as Facebook didn't enter the scene until she was eighteen. My years of mothering a teen girl were relatively easy compared to the onslaught of all the crazy so many moms are facing today.

Our culture grows increasingly perverted year by year. Anxiety and depression, comparison, and competition among teen girls are epidemic . . . unless we have a battle plan.

Prayer is the most potent battle plan I know. Nothing in the universe carries more weight, and nothing else will so profoundly transform our girls' lives. Prayer is the essential ingredient to impact the life of your teen girl.

As moms, we are raising our girls to be bold as lions yet gentle as doves—polar opposites yet perfect partners. When our daughters know where their strength comes from, they are in the best position to grow into strong and courageous, kind and gentle women of God.

As she enters her teen years, your girl will face overwhelming feelings she isn't sure how to manage. Hurts will come, and anger, competition, and confusion will descend as she begins to deal with real-life issues like betrayal, offense, worry, and all the other enormous emotions teenage girls face daily. Teen girls need their moms more than ever.

It's imperative that we share the truth of the reality of what following Christ means, teaching them that there will be a price in fighting the current culture. If we want our girls to be warriors, to know their purpose, and to be an example of endurance and courage in the hard times, we must pray. It will become our holy habit in these holy hard times.

But how do we do it? I wish I had a book like *Praying for Teen Girls* when I was raising mine!

This beautiful book by Stacey Thacker is a wonderful resource of prayers to pray and verses to ponder. She shares the wisdom of a mom who has been through real-life struggles and hardships with her own teen girls. Her story is brimming over with humility, transparency, and grace.

Let *Praying for Teen Girls* be your guide as you travel the road of raising your own teen girls.

Kate Battistelli, author of
The God Dare and *Growing Great Kids*

INTRODUCTION

It hasn't happened in a few years. Mostly because of the current ages of my girls. But there was a day when we would all traipse into a grocery store or Walmart or something like that, and the four of them would trail behind me somewhat in age order. Inevitably, while I was putting one or two of them in the shopping cart and giving instructions to the others to stay close, someone would say to me over the tops of their heads, "Are all these girls yours?" I would usually smile and say, "Yes, they are." At this point the stranger among us would go into detail about how hard it is to raise girls and how they couldn't imagine having four.

Right in front of my girls.

I would like to tell you that this only happened once or twice. Or that I didn't have to bite my tongue every time it happened because I had a thing or two I'd like to have said. That simply isn't the case. Truthfully, being a mom of four daughters has drawn a certain attention to my life that I didn't expect and probably haven't navigated perfectly. Even after more than twenty-five years of being a girl mom, I have much to learn.

One valuable lesson I have learned is that prayer is not optional. Maybe it's because I clearly see my lack, or maybe it's because I love my daughters so very much. I simply know that I need to partner with God on this journey. And prayer, for most of my life, has been a lifeline to me. It has been the way I have held on to God, especially when I didn't know what else to do.

I hear a lot of people say prayer is a last resort. And maybe it is at times. I think our stubbornness has a lot to do with how quickly we are willing to go to our knees. But prayer really is a relationship with the One who made our girls and loves them more than we do. He knows and loves us too. And having that kind of everyday access is a gift we can't ever grow out of. I know I need God more today with my twenty-five, twenty-two, eighteen, and fifteen-year-old girls than I did ten years ago. And I don't see that changing anytime soon.

Are you tired? Are you finding it hard to have conversations with your teen girl? Has she become a lot like you or a total stranger? Is she facing a bully at school? Has her friend group dropped her without so much as a wave goodbye? Do you want her to be strong but retain the softness you know is in there somewhere, even if she only lets you see it when she wants you to buy her Starbucks on the way to school? Does she doubt her worth? Is she standing on the edge of a beautiful future and just about ready to fly? Is she ready? Are you?

So, here is what I'm suggesting: Let's gather our courage as moms and grab on to the hem of the Lord's garment with all we have and pray. Let's stop trying to figure it all out and, instead, let it all out at the feet of the One who has the power to change not only our girls but our hearts as well.

Let's pray for our teen girls.

I think God wants us to. How do I know this? One of my favorite Bible verses on prayer is found in Psalm 116:2 (NLT): "Because he bends down to listen, I will pray as long as I have breath!" Can you picture Him now? He isn't sitting back cross-armed with headphones on, ignoring you. The God of heaven is leaning down toward you in a posture of gracious invitation to pray until your breath dies out on your lips because you have nothing else to say. And then guess what happens?

> And the Holy Spirit helps us in our weakness. For example, we don't know what God wants us to pray for. But the Holy Spirit prays for us with groanings that cannot be expressed in words.
>
> Romans 8:26 NLT

The Spirit prays for us. This really is a win-win situation. We pray, He listens. And when we don't have any more prayer words, He prays for us anyway.

I don't want you to think that this is going to be easy. I promise you the minute you set your mind to do this, the enemy (who hates prayer) will distract you. He will keep you busy. And tired. And frustrated. He might even start to mess with your family in small ways. Or big ones. But here is the thing: If you do this, and if you persevere, I happen to think that you will see God moving in ways you hadn't imagined He would. It may not happen today, but I do believe it will happen. For God "is able to do immeasurably more than all we ask or imagine" (Ephesians 3:20).

Regardless of what the stranger at Walmart thinks.

And if you don't know what to pray, keep reading. But by all means, let's pray. He is bending down to listen.

Looking Forward,
Stacey

HOW TO USE THIS BOOK

My favorite books have notes written in the margins, high-lighted dog-eared pages, and a coffee stain or two. They have a permanent place on my desk next to my Bible. I reach for them almost daily. And I confess, if someone asks to borrow them, I smile and say, "You know, let me buy you a copy for you to keep instead." This may sound generous, but in reality, I don't like to be separated from books I love. Maybe it is something like the stuffed animals my girls used to carry everywhere with them. They are like familiar friends and tell a part of my story I'd rather not loan out. Besides, I know they are going to *love* it anyway and will want to have their own copy with their own notes and coffee-stained pages.

I hope this book becomes one of your favorite prayer resources. I hope you wear it out and fold back the cover so the crease makes it even more usable. I hope you scribble answers to your prayers in the margins and take pictures of pages you want to share with your friends. I hope you reach for it every day and you read it with your Bible open and underline your favorite verses with a coordinating pen so you know these verses are prayers for your teen girl.

And if someone asks to borrow it, buy them a copy instead.

Part One: What to Pray for Yourself

Part One of this book is for you—the prayer warrior—to prepare your own heart. I have found over the years that when my heart is leaning toward the Lord, our conversations just flow better. There are two chapters with ten prayers each for you to pray over yourself. Which reminds me, it is absolutely essential to pray for yourself. Prayer is, at its core, a relationship with the Lord. Your prayer life will be a rich back-and-forth conversation as you talk to Him about your teen girl. So before you do that, talk to Him about your own struggles, needs, and fears. I chose the topics of humility (sorry this one is a bit painful) and transformation (because every one of us needs to grow in some way).

Start here, return often, and prepare your heart to fight for your girl.

Part Two: What to Pray for Your Teen Girl

The second part of this book includes seven prayer themes to pray through for your teen girl. Each chapter has ten passages to choose from as well. The prayer themes have been chosen with your teens in mind. They are general but strategic. I have written what I call a pep talk before the prayers in each chapter. I feel like sometimes you just need a reminder of why you are praying and what is at stake. I wish we could do this over coffee with our books open between us (see the next part for an idea along those lines). Perhaps we can utilize the good side of social media for that idea to have any chance of making it. Follow @prayingforteengirls on Instagram and we can get that going as best we can.

What you can do on your own is pray through one theme each day. Pick a verse or two from the end of each chapter to focus on. Add an alarm to your phone and pray throughout the day. Pray after you drop your teen girl off at school, or as you are going to sleep at night. I could have probably picked three times as many prayer themes, but I thought we have enough to keep us busy these days. Keeping it concise will help you make consistent progress in these key areas of your teen girl's life.

You might also ask your teen girl which area she needs prayer in right now. Ask her to pick a prayer theme, and then commit to praying for her every day until she asks for a different area of her life to be covered in prayer. You know what I think? I think she will be grateful you cared enough to ask. I think she will feel loved and known when she sees you with your book open and your head bowed.

Start a *Praying for Teen Girls* Prayer Cohort

If you know a teen girl, you know moms, grandmas, and mentors of teen girls. I'm guessing they are feeling like you do right now. I would be willing to bet they would love some encouragement and company as they pray for their teen girls too. You could text them, tag them on Facebook, or pull them aside at church and say, "Hey, I'm starting a small group to pray for our teen girls. Want to join?" They will either tell you they don't have time or they will tear up immediately and say, "Yes, sign me up." The former may come around eventually, but the latter will be your people. The way you run your prayer cohort (*group* is a simpler name, but I just like to be fancy and say words like *cohort*) is up to you. I would suggest a basic plan:

1. Plan to meet in person at the beginning.
2. Send out links to buy the book or buy them for the group yourself.

3. Read one chapter per week for nine weeks.

4. Have a weekly check-in. You can do it in person or on your phone (apps like GroupMe, Marco Polo, WhatsApp, or Voxer work great for this type of communication).

5. Share the names of your teen girls with each other. Pray for one other teen girl besides your own each week.

6. Meet at the end of the nine weeks to share what God has done in your lives.

7. Repeat.

I heard someone say once, "Nothing makes you love a person more than praying for them." I think you can also say, "Nothing makes you love a person more than praying *with* them." Your prayer cohort might just be your favorite part of your already crazy busy week.

Whatever you decide to do, I'd love to hear from you. Drop me an email, DM me on Instagram, or pull me to the side at church. Know that I'm right alongside you. I'm praying not only for you and your teen girls, but I'm praying for my own.

And I will not stop.

PART ONE

WHAT TO PRAY FOR
YOURSELF

1

LORD, SHOW ME
HOW TO WALK IN HUMILITY

Humility is simply the habit which prepares the soul for living
on trust.[1]

Andrew Murray, *Humility*

I remember it like it was yesterday. I was sitting in a wheelchair
curbside watching my husband pull our car into the nearest
parking place. The hospital orderly leaned down and said, "Sit
tight while we get everything ready for your ride home."

I didn't move except to cast a sideways glance to the bundle
of sweetness in my arms. I whispered more to her than anyone
in particular, "Do they know I'm leaving with you? Because
this feels risky. Me. You. Your dad. None of us know what we
are doing."

My firstborn daughter didn't have much to say about my lack
of confidence. She was sleeping soundly and trying not to be
disturbed by the early fall sunlight coming through the trees.

Trust me, though, as the weeks wore on, she had plenty to say about my inexperience as a new mom. I prayed long prayers during those never-ending nights, wondering how I was going to be a good mom if I didn't ever get any sleep.

By the time her three sisters joined us over the next ten years, I somewhat found my footing as a mom. I knew all about reading aloud to my girls, when they should be walking, what they should and shouldn't be eating, and how we would educate them. Oh, I was exhausted from the constantness of the early mothering years, but I was no longer inexperienced. My desperate prayers for guidance waned. I looked around at other moms, compared myself aplenty to what they were doing, and said to myself, "I should know how to do this by now. I'm a mom to four girls. I don't need to ask for help."

And for the most part I didn't. I worked harder, I read more books, and I listened to other seasoned moms. I smiled and said "I'm fine" when someone asked how I was doing. But in truth I wasn't fine at all. I was a weary mom, and I hid it well—until a hurricane blew through my Central Florida town and unraveled me once and for all. Empty, I prayed, "Lord, I'm not fine. I can't do this on my own." His response was surprising to me. He said, "I know. I've been waiting for you to realize that. Now, take a deep breath and write through it."

Humility in that season looked like a blog post I shared with the world. It involved me being willing to say it out loud first. It looked like swallowing my pride, opening my heart, and letting it bleed on the page. It meant being undone in front of others who thought I had it all together. What surprised me the most was that it resonated deeply with so many women. As it turns out, there were thousands. I kept writing, taking that message to the next level, wrote more than a few books, and shared hope with the world. All because I finally let humility find its place in my heart and empty me of me.

I'd like to tell you that the process of emptying me of me only needed to happen once. But that would make this book a fictional story, and that is most definitely not the case. We are here to prime the pump for prayer. And, as you will see, humility seems to be the best first step in the process. Maybe that is a dealbreaker for you. Maybe you are thinking, *Hey, I picked up this book because my teen girl is driving me crazy. I am at the end of my rope, and I need her to get with the program before I lose my mind.* I understand. I am all about the quick fix too. But over the years, I've learned and relearned that at the heart of prayer is our relationship with God. We have a beautiful invitation to learn from Him, pour out our hearts, and listen for His instructions. He can and will partner with us as we pray for the teen girls in our lives. But that doesn't mean that He will overlook what is happening in our hearts.

A Mom Who Had Great Faith

We probably would use words like *desperate* and *determined*. Others might say she was *audacious* and *annoying*. Either way, one thing is clear: When this Canaanite mother heard that Jesus was in town, she made it her mission to get herself to Him. She was not about to miss her opportunity and the chance that if she could get near enough to Jesus, He would grant her request.

> And Jesus went away from there and withdrew to the district of Tyre and Sidon. And behold, a Canaanite woman from that region came out and was crying, "Have mercy on me, O Lord, Son of David; my daughter is severely oppressed by a demon."
>
> Matthew 15:21–22 ESV

Jesus spent most of His time in Judea and Galilee, preaching the gospel and news of His coming kingdom to the Jewish people. We only see Him taking the occasional trip to other places. Both Matthew and Mark share this encounter with the Canaanite mother and point out that Jesus went away to this region, though not specifically where He went. Maybe He was hiding out, maybe He was waiting, or maybe He was tired of arguing with faithless teachers who were determined to catch Him in a war of words. The contrast of this Canaanite woman's faith (think of her people as the bitter enemy of Israel, who typically worshiped pagan gods and drew God's people into idolatry) is astounding. And loud. She did not say it softly. She shouted out, pleading for compassion and leaning boldly into the mercy of Jesus. She honored Him both as master and Messiah, stating quickly her one request for her daughter, who was oppressed by a demon and being constantly tormented.

Help her. I know you can.

"But he did not answer her a word. And his disciples came and begged him, saying, 'Send her away, for she is crying out after us,'" (Matthew 15:23 ESV). Initially Jesus' answer was silence. He didn't utter a word. Or a syllable. Or sigh. Or say anything.

Let me pause here because sometimes I wrestle with my pride and I finally get myself before Jesus to make my request and He answers me with silence too. I feel this pregnant pause before this woman in the very depths of my own mama-bear heart. I don't know if I feel incredibly seen or frustrated by this. Maybe, if I'm honest, I feel a little bit of both. She had done the hard work of getting there and finally being heard. What more could He want from her?

Jesus paused long enough for the disciples to interject (don't they always?). Now they were begging too. But for an entirely different reason. They were bothered. They wanted Him to deal with her. I don't know if they were in favor of her being sent on her way without getting what she sought or not. They had walked with Jesus long enough and witnessed His generally gracious response to those who sought Him earnestly. But they were not big fans of a foreign woman gaining His attention, just like the woman at the well—a Samaritan. Maybe they simply wanted her dealt with either way. She was His problem, not theirs.

Finally, Jesus speaks. "He answered, 'I was sent only to the lost sheep of the house of Israel.' But she came and knelt before him, saying, 'Lord, help me'" (Matthew 15:24–25 ESV). He verbally puts her off and denies her request. Oh, He tells her why and what for: His mission, which He has wholeheartedly accepted, is to the lost sheep of Israel. Translation: *My first priority is there, not here. Them, not you.*

Are you shocked by this? I am. This does not sound like my favorite version of Jesus. Isn't He love and kindness and compassion? If you believe social media, that is all He is. But He is more: He is the truth. He is holy. He is right. Always. Apparently, this Gentile mama is not deterred. She actually comes closer. She presses in. She goes low. She kneels before Him and says, once again, "Lord, help me."

The implication is this: *I can't. You can.*

Surely that will do it, right? Can she go lower? What else does He want from her? "And he answered, 'It is not right to take the children's bread and throw it to the dogs'" (Matthew 15:26 ESV).

Wait a minute. Did Jesus just call her a dog? Yes and no. The term He uses here isn't the typical slanderous remark most Jews used about Gentiles, which meant a wild, rabid, crazy animal. Jesus chooses a different word that is more like a pet or puppy. At this point, part of me wants to keep my ire up at this scene, but what Jesus is doing here is masterful. He is telling a story. He is drawing out her faith. He is using a proverbial statement, and she is going to meet His invitation with faith that will unsettle the entire audience. I even think He might have said it with a question in His eyes and a slight smile. Maybe He even quirked His brow to draw out her next phrase:

> She said, "Yes, Lord, yet even the dogs eat the crumbs that fall from their masters' table." Then Jesus answered her, "O woman, great is your faith! Be it done for you as you desire." And her daughter was healed instantly.
>
> Matthew 15:27–28 ESV

She agreed with Him that she was a dog. So, yes, she could go lower. In fact, she is a dog under the table of the chosen family. Though, I will add here that family pets who sit under tables with children eating a meal are really smart too. My dog, Derby, knows that if he is patient enough, and quick enough, whatever falls on the floor belongs to him. And honestly, I kind of appreciate that he is there and I don't have to sweep up after dinners most nights. For this woman, pride had no place and she didn't take no for an answer. She knew she had no other options, and so she clung to Jesus and what she knew without a doubt that He could do for her and her daughter. Leon Morris shares this commentary:

> This neat answer shows that the woman was not presuming on her position. She knew that she did not belong to Israel and thus had no claim as belonging to the chosen people. But surely there would be crumbs![2]

She did not ask for a seat at the table; she was only seeking crumbs. But she knew that even with the crumbs there were significant blessings. This wrecks me. Truly. Because in her I see what I am not. I clamor for a seat at the table, demanding my rights: *Answer my prayers, my way*. But she is humbly willing to accept the miniscule pieces that fall to the floor, and that is sufficient for her demon-possessed and tormented daughter to be set free. Why? Because the crumbs are from the hand of Jesus. And He always has the right provision to meet our needs.

Jesus' response is quick and enthusiastic. He holds her faith up as a testimony to the twelve and those who have gathered to witness the interchange. Which, as a side note, He only does previously one other time, with a centurion in Matthew 8 who asks for healing for his servant. And then her deepest desire—healing for her girl—is granted at that very hour.

Why We Resist Prayer

We probably all have our own version of the answer to why we resist prayer. My friend Brooke McGlothlin wisely says that prayer should be our "first and best response to motherhood."[3] She even wrote a whole book about it called *Praying Mom*. In that book she lists several reasons we don't pray, and every last one of them resonates with me. I gave part of my story to the chapter called, "I'm Exhausted from Trying to Trust God." Which is just another way of saying, "I'm tired from being so responsible."

Other women said they resisted prayer because they didn't know what to pray or if their prayers mattered. Some said they wanted to wait until they got their life together or their little ones got a little older and slept a little more. But if I look below the surface of each of these reasons, including my own, what I see is that ultimately, we think of prayer as a last resort. We treat it like a holy bailout to use when things get really, really bad. Why do we feel that way? Honestly, because we don't know who God is and what He has offered to us as His children. In the process, we shrink the size of our God, and we grow bigger in puffed-up pride, naturally assuming we are fine without Him.

"Outside of biblical faith, humility would be *lunacy*. Who wants *less* power, *less* prestige?"[4] Who wants to go lower? Who wants to be a dog under the table looking for crumbs? So we must look to Jesus and the example set before us:

> Have this mind among yourselves, which is yours in Christ Jesus, who, though he was in the form of God, did not count equality with God a thing to be grasped, but emptied himself, by taking the form of a servant, being born in the likeness of men. And being found in human form, he humbled himself by becoming obedient to the point of death, even death on a cross. Therefore God has highly exalted him and bestowed on him the name that is above every name, so that at the name of Jesus every knee should bow, in heaven and on earth and under the earth, and every tongue confess that Jesus Christ is Lord, to the glory of God the Father.
>
> Philippians 2:5–11 ESV

Over the past year I've been meditating on and memorizing this passage. It has humbled me over and over again. Jesus doesn't just say, "Hey, be humble." No, He went first. He set His rights aside, and instead He chose:

Emptiness

Servanthood

Humility

Obedience

Death on a cross

The further I work my way down this verse, the looser my grip on control of my life becomes. It is all kinds of unsettling. And yet, it reminds me that this type of life isn't possible without Him. I can't walk in humility on my own. It takes the mind of Christ in me, working in and through my surrender, to produce anything that remotely looks like humility in my own life. According to Erika Allen, author of the *ESV Prayer Journal: 30 Days on Humility*,

> The English words *humble* and *humility* are rooted in a Latin word that means *low*. When we view ourselves as low in comparison to others, we are on the path to Christlikeness, because humility allows other godly qualities to take root. Humility is the foundation upon which kindness, compassion, gentleness, mercy, and patience are built.[5]

Low means I'm on the path to being like Jesus. This is necessary whether I'm praying about my own life or the teen girls in my home, at school, or in my church. Do I want to see kindness and compassion in them? It had better be easy to spot in my life as well. Am I asking them to trust God as they step out in faith? If they don't see my hands firmly in the grip of Jesus, what on earth would possess them to obey Him when He leads them along the sometimes rocky path of life? Humility means I'm willing to ask Christ to first produce His life in me—way before I ask Him to do it for others.

Why Empty and Available Matters

Several years ago, my word for the year was *available*. It sounded good at the beginning of the year. I thought God would hand me book contracts, speaking assignments, and podcast interviews that would change the world. That wasn't exactly what happened. Pretty quickly I realized that *available* had a close cousin named *empty*. And God began the process of peeling back the layers of my heart to shine His light on what was hidden deep below the surface.

It was a habit of mine, when I saw *available* anywhere, to pause and pray. I would say, *Hey, Lord, there is my word for the year! What do you want to say to me?* One day I was driving down one of my favorite roads, which led through the quaint part of town where I love to grab coffee with friends, and I saw a building with a sign that read "Available" and a phone number to call for more information. As I drove on toward home, I saw another sign. And another. And another. They all said "Available" on them. Perhaps my favorite part of town was going through a much-needed rebirth. I smiled and said, *Okay, Lord. I see it. What are you trying to say?* And in the stillness of the moment a question popped into my head:

Why are those buildings all available?

And as I stopped at the next stoplight it hit me. *Because they are empty.*

I knew it was time for a rebirth in my heart as well. Hidden just beneath the surface for me was years of feeling hidden, hurt, and hopeless amid several life-altering events. I was surviving but I wasn't thriving. I was available, but I was by no means empty. I still had a firm grip on my version of the story I wanted to live, and I didn't want to let go.

Jesus didn't cling to His right to be God. Though He was. He poured Himself out. He was available to be used by God and took on the form of a servant. He didn't demand His will. He emptied Himself. And then, He went even further. He was willing to die a horrible death so that He could save us. What did Jesus willingly pray just before He went to the cross?

> And going a little farther he fell on his face and prayed, saying, "My Father, if it be possible, let this cup pass from me; nevertheless, not as I will, but as you will."
>
> Matthew 26:39 ESV

God's will was for Him to die. He did that for you. He did that for me. He did that for the teen girls in our lives. And if Jesus emptied Himself and depended on God, how can we not do the same? Our prayers, clothed in the habit of humility, can become an offering instead of a negotiation. They demonstrate our absolute trust in His will being accomplished in His way.

What is God's response to a humble and willing heart? Scripture says that God opposes the proud but pours out grace on the truly humble (see James 4:6). As we take this journey of prayer together, we are going to need all the grace we can get. Aren't you glad He has already promised it? Take the grace, my friend.

Before You Check Out

I know this is hard. But I also know how much you love the teen girl in your life. I know, like that Gentile mom, you are willing to do anything to get your girl to Jesus. But can I tell you something? That fierceness with which you love her—Jesus sees you, and He loves you like that too. And before you close this book and say, "This is too hard. Thank you, but no," I want to tell you one of the most humbling stories of my life.

A few years ago, my family was hit with one loss after another. In a short three-year time frame my dad lost his battle with cancer, my almost nine-year-old daughter was diagnosed with a severe chronic illness, and my husband had a sudden cardiac arrest. These trials sent me in anguish to my knees repeatedly. I was very familiar with my bathroom floor. I don't think you can get much lower—maybe the dog under the table is comparable? I found this an appropriate position for prayer. But often I would just sit and weep as quietly as I could because I didn't want to scare my girls. There were days I wasn't sure He was even there, with me on the bathroom floor. I wondered if

He saw me. If He cared. If He was going to answer my desperate prayers anytime soon.

During that time, not once but several times, God put people in my path who would ask just the right questions, have words of encouragement, or reach out to me with a text or written note. They would typically say something to the effect of, "Hey, Stacey, God brought you to mind today, and I want you to know that I'm praying for you and your family." Often the encouragement would arrive with a financial gift that covered a need I hadn't told anyone about but God. This went on for a couple of years. Consistently. It only stopped when I started working full time at my church. It was like manna from heaven that ceased once we were in our own personal promised land.

I'm not sure I will ever view prayer the same way again. It isn't about me coming to God and demanding my rights. It is about recognizing I am lost without Him. Prayer leaves pride on the floor of the bathroom and under the table and picks up the crumbs of all-sufficient grace Jesus offers instead. Humility says through tears, "I trust you, Jesus." And He scoops us up in His arms and says, "I see you. I love you. I'm going to take care of your family."

And He does.

Every single time.

PRAYERS FOR HUMILITY

Philippians 2:5–8—"In your relationships with one another, have the same mindset as Christ Jesus: Who, being in very nature God, did not consider equality with God something to be used to his own advantage; rather, he made himself nothing by taking the very nature of a servant, being made in human likeness. And being found in appearance as a man, he humbled himself by becoming obedient to death—even death on a cross!"

> **PRAYER:** Father, when I am tempted to think highly of myself, remind me of the attitude of Christ, who was equal with God but didn't use it as an advantage. Instead, He laid aside His glory and emptied Himself to become a humble servant. He obeyed you to the point of death. I want that same Spirit to be seen in my life as well. In Jesus' name, Amen.

James 4:10—"Humble yourselves before the Lord, and he will lift you up."

> **PRAYER:** Father, humility is my job, lifting me up is your job. And even if you don't, I will still honor you. In Jesus' name, Amen.

1 Peter 5:6–7—"Humble yourselves, therefore, under God's mighty hand, that he may lift you up in due time. Cast all your anxiety on him because he cares for you."

> **PRAYER:** Father, by your grace I set aside my pride of self-promotion and will wait on you to lift me up in your appropriate timing. And while I wait, I will give you all my worries because I know you are concerned for me. In Jesus' name, Amen.

Proverbs 3:5–6—"Trust in the LORD with all your heart and lean not on your own understanding; in all your ways submit to him, and he will make your paths straight."

> **PRAYER:** Father, right here and right now I am telling you I want to trust you with all of my heart. I don't want to try to figure out the future on my own. I will put you first, look to you always, and trust you will remove any obstacles that might come my way. In Jesus' name, Amen.

Isaiah 66:1–2—"This is what the LORD says: 'Heaven is my throne, and the earth is my footstool. Where is the house you will build for me? Where will my resting place be? Has not my hand made all these things, and so they came into being?' declares the LORD. 'These are the ones I look on with favor: those who are humble and contrite in spirit, and who tremble at my word.'"

> **PRAYER:** Father, you truly are above all things. As one who desires your favor, I reverently submit myself to your Word and will do what it says. In Jesus' name, Amen.

Matthew 26:39—"Going a little farther, he fell with his face to the ground and prayed, 'My Father, if it is possible, may this cup be taken from me. Yet not as I will, but as you will.'"

> **PRAYER:** Father, I'm grateful that Jesus doesn't ask me to pray something He wasn't willing to pray Himself. So I say in agreement with Him, "not as I will, but as you will," Lord. In Jesus' name, Amen.

Matthew 5:5—"Blessed are the meek, for they will inherit the earth."

> **PRAYER:** Father, give me a heart that is kind and self-controlled. Then and only then will I have something of true worth that money can't buy. In Jesus' name, Amen.

Proverbs 11:12—"Whoever derides their neighbor has no sense, but the one who has understanding holds their tongue."

> **PRAYER:** Father, when I feel the urge to say something that will not be beneficial to others, give me discretion to stay silent instead. In Jesus' name, Amen.

Psalm 40:1—"I waited patiently for the LORD; he turned to me and heard my cry."

PRAYER: Father, teach me to wait expectantly for you to speak before I move forward with a matter. Thank you for not making me wait any longer than necessary. In Jesus' name, Amen.

2 Corinthians 8:9—"For you know the grace of our Lord Jesus Christ, that though he was rich, yet for your sake he became poor, so that you through his poverty might become rich."

PRAYER: Father, as rich as Jesus was, He gave it all up so I would be abundantly blessed by His grace. I pray that your generosity of selfless living would be evident in my life as well. In Jesus' name, Amen.

2

LORD, I BELIEVE. HELP MY UNBELIEF.

I can think of nothing great that is also easy. Prayer must be, then, one of the hardest things in the world. To admit that prayer is very hard, however, can be encouraging. If you struggle greatly in this, you are not alone.[1]

Timothy Keller

Not too long ago I was invited to be interviewed for my book *Threadbare Prayer*. During that season I was doing several interviews a day on the topic of prayer. Most were recorded, which helped me tremendously. The interviewer typically would say to me, "I want you to know this interview is being recorded and can be edited. So if you say anything you want to change or fix, you can simply say, 'I'd like to cut that and start over,' and our producer will take that out completely." Editors are amazing. Especially when you find yourself suddenly nervous to speak publicly about a subject that is near and dear to your heart.

This interview was different for two reasons. First of all, it was live, and no form of sound editing was offered. Second, it was not only live, it was live on Facebook. Nevertheless, I settled into this live interview and had a wonderful time with the host, whose name was Angie. At one point she asked me a question that I can't remember. What I do remember is my answer, which went something like this:

"You know, Angie, I feel like an unlikely prayer warrior. I mean, if I had been picking someone to write a prayer book, I would not have picked me. I have prayed with people who are clearly prayer warriors. They pray fiercely courageous prayers, and they know how to wield that weapon well. I've never felt that way about my prayer life." (You know them too, right?)

Angie didn't hesitate. She challenged me. Live. On Facebook. She said, "I disagree with you." (Hello awkward moment!) "You are a prayer warrior because you are in the battle and have not given up." I sort of agreed with her on that point but was caught up in my own head when she added with a smile, "Oh, even if that is true, God never uses unlikely people. Nope. You can't find any of those in Scripture." Well, okay then. Angie, you make an excellent point. Or rather two excellent points. I conceded with a smile and thanked her for the reminder.

Maybe you don't feel like a prayer warrior either. I hope it helps to know that I still struggle with the term, though I'm seeing more and more the truth that God can and will use unlikely people like me and you and countless others in the pages of His Word. In fact, I think He delights in doing so.

What Is on the Other Side of Prayer

If humility is the best first step in prayer, then our personal heart transformation might just be one of the main goals. You may be thinking, *Wait, I'm praying for my teen girl, and my goals are about God transforming her.* I get that. I really do. But what I have learned about prayer over the years is that God is more concerned with the state of our relationship with Him than our requests. Oh, He will answer your prayers. But what happens in between is that we grow closer to Him in the process. We learn about His heart. And more and more, little by little, we start to want what He wants for us and others.

Prayer becomes like a beautiful dance that we lean into and let Him lead. He takes a step, and we follow. But the process of being okay with that type of trust relationship takes time and patience that often our teen girl crisis situations don't always seem to allow. Yet God knows our hearts and needs before we utter a word. I don't think He holds out on us until we get with the program. All I'm saying is that He deeply cares about what is going on inside of us, and He wants to make sure that we don't miss everything He has for us as His children as we pray for those we love as well.

I Believe—Help Me Believe More

Have you ever stopped to think about how many stories there are about parents who come to Jesus to request help for their children? This past year I have been taking notice as I read and reread the Gospels in various order and versions.[2] People who had problems came to get help. They were also transformed in the process.

The father in Mark 9:14–29 deserves a medal. Not only is he dealing with a demon-possessed child who is mute and throwing himself on the ground, but he also must overcome the disciples' inability to help him. You may have noticed, there are several stories about demon possession like this in the Gospels. It may make you feel a little bit uncomfortable. I find it interesting that it is simply stated without any fanfare. In much the same way I avoid scary movies or books that keep me awake at night, this may feel darker than you care to consider. Remember, though,

Jesus is the light of the world, and what He does in this story is show us what it looks like to bring light into an impossible situation. Keep in mind, He is never not in control.

What amuses me (if I may be so bold) is that there have been times I've looked at my teenagers and wondered what in the world possessed them to do something. Now, I'm not saying they were actually possessed. But there are times when they seem to abandon all reason and can't have a normal conversation with me. This story in the Gospels is kind of like that but worse. Also, the disciples, for the most part, are teenagers. So, what we have here is a father trying to find relief for his troubled son and a group of teenagers who have no idea what to do. I don't know about you, but this is exactly the type of story that sets my heart at ease and reminds me I am not alone.

When Jesus enters the situation, everything shifts. He quickly asks the father of the child, "How long has this been happening to him?" and the father says, "From childhood" (Mark 9:21 ESV). This simple question ministers deeply to me. I have prayed long and hard over certain areas for my girls. The fact that Jesus wants to acknowledge to this father the length of time he has been struggling shows me that Jesus cares. He knows when we are at our wits' end, and He knows when we need rest. We don't know how old the boy is in this story, but I get the idea that it has been several years. This father has had years of feeling helpless while his son has been tormented and his life threatened. Over and over again.

Do you know what it is like? Have you gone to your knees more than once and cried out for help, not knowing when it was going to come? This parent felt the same way. I can imagine his next words to Jesus were through tears or at least frustration. I love the way *The Message* phrases his words directed to Jesus: "If you can do anything, do it. Have a heart and help us!" (Mark

9:22 MSG). As it turns out, appealing to the incredible heart of Jesus was the key that unlocked the father's heart as well.

> "'If you can'?" said Jesus. "Everything is possible for one who believes." Immediately the boy's father exclaimed, "I do believe; help me overcome my unbelief!"
>
> Mark 9:23–24

I don't think the father had zero faith or one-hundred-percent unbelief. I think he had to have at least a shred of belief to bring his son to Jesus in the first place. I identify with that small faith. I believe in asking for things in prayer that I know I can't fix on my own. But sometimes my little bit of faith falls so short compared to what I think Jesus wants from me. Lucky for me and this father, little is much when God is in it. The question here isn't if Jesus can heal this boy, the question is whether the father believes Jesus can do it. I love his humble and desperate response.

I believe, but I have some doubts. Heal my unbelief.

And here, in the company of a faithless crowd who didn't have the desperation this father had, Jesus did both. He healed the boy and the father with a simple command fueled by prayer.

My little bit of faith, a mustard seed at times, finds great encouragement here in the presence of a father who admitted, "Hey, Jesus, I have some doubts. But I don't want to." Prayer is the place to deliver your own doubts to Jesus and watch as He does impossible things in the lives of our teen girls and transforms our hearts as well.

What Happens When We Pray

No one said prayer was easy. I for one am grateful that the late Tim Keller acknowledged that prayer is hard. I have often felt exhausted when I've prayed. Sometimes it seems like I've gone rounds in a wrestling match. Other times I have closed my eyes to pray and drawn a complete blank. Or been distracted by my to-do list. Much of the time, I feel like I'm shooting blind arrows out into space, wondering if anyone is listening. But at the same time, when I take note of the sometimes small changes in my own heart, I can clearly see that who I was when I started is not who I have become.

First, prayer has the unique ability to stop my downward fall into the pit of despair. It arrests my free fall and launches me toward higher God-directed thoughts. Romans 12:2 calls this process of transformation the renewing of our minds and carries the idea of a "renovation" or "complete change for the better."[3] It doesn't matter what I'm talking to Jesus about; somewhere in the conversation I pause and change my direction. It might only be a baby step toward His perspective, but even a tiny step is an improvement.

Second, and very much related to my mind being restored, peace begins to flow like a river over my whole being when I pray. Just like Jesus' conversation with Martha in the midst of her busy kitchen, He says to my worrisome heart, "Stacey. Stacey, you are bothered about so many things. Focus on what truly matters." And though I don't have a clue how His Spirit accomplishes it, peace grows because my focus is not on the problem but the one I'm having the conversation with. Jesus has promised me that when I invite Him into any situation, He brings peace that confounds the world (see John 14:27).

Something else that happens when we pray is that we gain the gift of endurance. Truthfully, I want God's will, but I secretly want it on my own timetable. I want it now. Or yesterday. Waiting is hard, and prayer is filled with it. To top it off, the Bible tells us in Romans 5 that endurance (or perseverance) is part of the classroom of suffering:

Not only so, but we also glory in our sufferings, because we know that suffering produces perseverance; perseverance, character; and character, hope. And hope does not put us to shame, because God's love has been poured out into our hearts through the Holy Spirit, who has been given to us.

Romans 5:3–5

Have you had seasons of suffering that seem to settle in your soul? I would be willing to guess that you are praying pretty much constantly. I know nothing makes me pray more than suffering. Somehow, while I'm praying, God produces a steadiness that gives way to character and hope because His Spirit is being poured out in our hearts. Hard? Yes! Worth it? Most definitely. Think of it this way—if praying were a sport, it would be a marathon, and running it would take years of commitment and training. But in the end, the run would be all the sweeter for the gain of a body and soul marked by perseverance. I want that, don't you?

A Not-So-Silly Phenomenon

One of my favorite things to do is to look at photographs of couples who have been married for decades. Do you know what I see more often than not? I see two people who have started to look alike. They have similar laugh lines and smiles. They are dressed alike and are deeply connected. If you catch an interview with one such couple, you will even notice that they have the unique ability to finish each other's sentences. You should also know there is a thread on social media for people who look like their pets. I'm not saying that is the goal, mind you, just that there are some who take so much pride in their pint-sized companions that they look like family. The time we spend with others rubs off on us, and hopefully that is more sweet than scary.

I was reminded recently of a story in Acts 4 that is along the same lines. Peter and John, two of the most prominent members of Jesus' disciples, were speaking to the people about all they had seen and heard. Most significant was that they were talking about Jesus' death, burial, and resurrection. The leaders were so angry they put both Peter and John in jail. But that didn't stop the message from effectively drawing around five thousand men to believe in Jesus. This confused the leaders, who themselves were educated men. They couldn't figure out how in the world these two fishermen were able to teach with such authority.

But Peter couldn't help but speak. He was filled with the Holy Spirit and went on teaching these learned men. You know Peter, right? The same guy who denied Jesus and fled during His trial (see Luke 22:54–62). That guy. He preached a powerful message about how to be saved through Jesus. I don't know if any of the leaders in front of Peter and John were moved by what he said. Likely they were not because they told them to stop teaching. But they noticed something else they could not disregard:

> When they saw the courage of Peter and John and realized that they were unschooled, ordinary men, they were astonished and they took note that these men had been with Jesus.
>
> Acts 4:13

They were fascinated by the confident courage on display in two ordinary men who didn't have a fraction of their academic knowledge. Do you know what they attributed such courage to? Peter and John were friends of Jesus. They spent time with Him. Do you know what these same men saw in Jesus? Confident authority—courage. Jesus had it in spades. He oozed it. He didn't back down. He was not afraid. He taught with the same authority that now came from His disciples.

I wonder at times if Peter and John were equally astonished when they heard themselves preaching with such courage. They had to know the source of that courage wasn't from them. It was because they were friends of Jesus. They spent time with Him. They watched Him and listened to Him and built a relationship with Him so that they started looking and sounding like Him too.

I don't know about you, but I want that same type of transformation in my own life. Me? Courageous? Yes. And not because I am bold and brave on my own, but because I have spent days, weeks, and even years on my knees letting the courage of Jesus infuse every part of my heart, and I haven't quit asking for Him to cure the small doubts that try to keep me from asking for more.

Jesus, I believe. Help my unbelief.

PRAYERS FOR TRANSFORMATION

Hebrews 4:12—"For the word of God is alive and active. Sharper than any double-edged sword, it penetrates even to dividing soul and spirit, joints and marrow; it judges the thoughts and attitudes of the heart."

> **PRAYER:** Father, thank you that your Word is living and powerful. Let it cut to the deepest part of my heart so that it exposes my thoughts and motives. I ask that it will do something in me and through me that makes me more like you. In Jesus' name, Amen.

Romans 12:1–2—"Therefore, I urge you, brothers and sisters, in view of God's mercy, to offer your bodies as a living sacrifice, holy and pleasing to God—this is your true and proper worship. Do not conform to the pattern of this world, but be transformed by the renewing of your mind. Then you will be able to test and approve what God's will is—his good, pleasing and perfect will."

> **PRAYER**: Father, I give you my one ordinary life and ask you to use it for your glory. I don't want to look or act like the world. Please renovate me from the inside out, according to your life-giving Word. Give me the ability to see and know your good and perfect will. In Jesus' name, Amen.

2 Corinthians 3:18—"And we all, who with unveiled faces contemplate the Lord's glory, are being transformed into his image with ever-increasing glory, which comes from the Lord, who is the Spirit."

> **PRAYER**: Father, as I continue to look to you, keep transforming me little by little. When others see me, I pray I will look more and more like you. In Jesus' name, Amen.

Ephesians 4:22–24—"You were taught, with regard to your former way of life, to put off your old self, which is being corrupted by its deceitful desires; to be made new in the attitude of your minds; and to put on the new self, created to be like God in true righteousness and holiness."

> **PRAYER**: Father, today I need the reminder to completely put away my old self that is corrupt and useless to me now. Instead, I will take hold of my new and beautiful life that Christ made possible, which points to His righteousness and holiness as I walk with Him. In Jesus' name, Amen.

Colossians 4:2—"Devote yourselves to prayer, being watchful and thankful."

PRAYER: Father, I will continue to be steadfast and constant in prayer no matter what. I will keep my eyes wide open, looking for your answers, and will be thankful. In Jesus' name, Amen.

Acts 4:13—"When they saw the courage of Peter and John and realized that they were unschooled, ordinary men, they were astonished and they took note that these men had been with Jesus."

PRAYER: Father, I pray that when others see me and how I live for you, they will recognize that I have spent time with you. In Jesus' name, Amen.

Romans 5:3–5—"Not only so, but we also glory in our sufferings, because we know that suffering produces perseverance; perseverance, character; and character, hope. And hope does not put us to shame, because God's love has been poured out into our hearts through the Holy Spirit, who has been given to us."

PRAYER: Father, I know from experience that you use suffering to transform my character. I pray that you will use everything in my life—even hard things—to grow me into a steadfast, mature, hope-filled follower of you. In Jesus' name, Amen.

Mark 9:23–24—"'If you can'?" said Jesus. 'Everything is possible for one who believes.' Immediately the boy's father exclaimed, 'I do believe; help me overcome my unbelief!'"

PRAYER: Father, all things are possible when we believe in you. Help me believe more and overcome any doubts that surface when I pray. In Jesus' name, Amen.

Philippians 4:6–7—"Do not be anxious about anything, but in every situation, by prayer and petition, with thanksgiving, present your requests to God. And the peace of God, which transcends all understanding, will guard your hearts and your minds in Christ Jesus."

> **PRAYER:** Father, I confess that my first response is to worry about all the things. But you tell me instead to pray, be thankful, and make my petition to you. When I do that, you trade my worries for overwhelming peace and promise to protect my mind like a military guard. God, I want that today and ask that you make it so in my life. In Jesus' name, Amen.

Psalm 139:23–24—"Search me, God, and know my heart; test me and know my anxious thoughts. See if there is any offensive way in me, and lead me in the way everlasting."

> **PRAYER:** Father, I invite you to search my heart and examine my thoughts. Point out to me if there is anything not in alignment with your Word—worry, sin, or dark thoughts. I want to give those to you and ask you to guide me on the path that leads to life. In Jesus' name, Amen.

PRAYERS AND NOTES

PART TWO

WHAT TO PRAY FOR YOUR TEEN GIRL

3

LORD, PURSUE HER HEART

Live from the abundant place that you are loved, and you won't find yourself begging others for scraps of love.[1]

Lysa TerKeurst

Teen girls have been having a cultural moment. Clad in pink and flocking to the movie theater, they embraced their inner Barbie and launched her dreamhouse world to the top of the box office mountain. Coming-of-age series on Prime Video tell us how normal it is to go from barely noticeable to the prettiest girl in the breath of a summer. And unless you've been living on Mars, you have surely noticed them dancing, posting, and raising their hands and friendship bracelets while Taylor Swift (a teen sensation herself some years ago) sang her way across the world, packing stadiums and single-handedly influencing the economy to the tune of billions of dollars in revenue.

And yet, teen girls are also in crisis. According to a recent study published by the CDC, teen girls are facing a mental health epidemic and faring much worse than their teen boy counterparts: "Nearly 3 in 5 (57%) U.S. teen girls felt persistently sad or hopeless in 2021—double that of boys, representing a nearly 60% increase and the highest level reported over the past decade."[2]

These numbers are startling. They don't seem to match what we see every day when we pick up our phones. Unless of course you are close to a teen girl or several. You most likely aren't shaking your head at all at news like this. Researcher Anita Slomski writes,

> Child and reproductive psychiatrist Misty Richards puts it bluntly: "Our teen girls are not okay." The program director for UCLA's Child and Adolescent Psychiatry Fellowship recently cared for a girl who attempted suicide after receiving a college rejection letter. "Her self-worth was measured in achievement and external accolades, and she felt she couldn't be anything other than perfect," Richards said in an interview. "We've had to create a backup call system in the emergency department at UCLA to get more help for the numbers of teenagers— specifically teen girls with suicide attempts or serious injurious behavior like cutting—who are in absolute crisis. We've never seen numbers like this before."[3]

As the mother of at least one teen girl for the past decade myself, I can tell you these numbers tell a story no mother wants to hear. Or witness. I remember my pastor saying one time, "When you have little kids, they have little problems. When you have big kids, they have big problems." He was right. I can tell you there is a drastic difference between holding and healing my girls during their toddler years and wrapping my arms around my taller-than-me teen girl who has had her heart broken— again. This is not easy. And though it would be tempting here to dive into the negatives of social media (we will talk about that in a later chapter), I want to start in the most precious place—her heart. It is worth fighting for, and praying for her heart might be your most persistent prayer for your teen girl.

The God Who Sees Me

Our teen girls are a lot like us. They long to be seen and known. They want likes, followers, and friends. There isn't anything inherently wrong with those desires. Some would say they are part of being human. But problems arise when these desires take top shelf in their hearts and create a sense of self-worth that rises and falls when desires are met or unmet, as they inevitably are. How do we help our teen girl understand her true worth and how amazing she is?

One of my favorite characters from *The Chronicles of Narnia* series by C. S. Lewis is Lucy. Throughout the series with the Pevensie siblings we watch her grow from a child with imaginative faith to a grown-up girl with depth of feelings. In the middle teen years, she struggles. As we all do. One of my favorite scenes from the movie adaptation several years ago features this struggle. She finds a book of spells and wishes she was someone else. Lucy didn't have social media, but she had a big sister who was beautiful. By comparison, Lucy felt awkward and unseen. She wished her life away because she didn't understand her part in the greater story or understand her value. In the dream sequence, Aslan speaks to her as she looks in the mirror. When she looks away, she doesn't see him.[4] I love this subtle nod to the idea that when we are straining to see who we are, we don't get the full picture apart from the Lord. Paul also paints a similar picture in the letter to the church at Corinth:

> When I was a child, I talked like a child, I thought like a child, I reasoned like a child. When I became a man, I put the ways of childhood behind me. For now we see only a reflection as in

a mirror; then we shall see face to face. Now I know in part; then I shall know fully, even as I am fully known.

1 Corinthians 13:11–12

We have limited perspectives no matter if we are thirteen or thirty. We can only see a tiny glimpse of who we are becoming. The process can be beautiful and painful. The key for a teen girl is knowing that the part of the mirror she sees today is obscured and difficult to understand without being fully known by the one who created her in His perfect image. Fortunately for her, just like for Lucy, He sees her clearly and pursues her heart with the fierceness of a roaring lion.

How do I know this? Other than being the mom of four teen girls and myself having been that girl looking in the mirror daily for glimpses of my true worth, I am also a self-proclaimed Bible nerd who loves to spend hours looking up words in the original Hebrew and Greek languages of the Bible. I get excited and text my girlfriends when I find something I didn't see before. I come alive when the Word opens before me in the early morning hours as I sip giant cups of coffee and listen to worship music. I also have a favorite name of God that is tucked in the story of a young woman who was in the middle of a messy situation and decided it just wasn't worth working it out—so she ran. Her name was Hagar, and she most definitely did not know her worth or that she was worth being noticed by God. You can find her story in Genesis 16.

How she got to where she was is shocking. She was a slave given to her mistress's husband to bear a child on her behalf. When nature took its course, disagreements arose between the slave and the mistress. Okay, so that is not so shocking, and to be honest, running away probably made a whole lot of sense to her at the time. But who found her in the middle of her all-out run while stopping in a desert place is even more incredible:

The angel of the LORD found Hagar near a spring in the desert; it was the spring that is beside the road to Shur. And he said, "Hagar, slave of Sarai, where have you come from, and where are you going?"

Genesis 16:7–8

Found. She doesn't deny her scandalous history or her bleak future. Surprisingly the messenger tells her to go back but gives her a promise that she will not only have a son but a big family as well. For a woman alone and in her situation, this would have been hard to comprehend. Her response is in the form of a prayer, and she says, "'You are the God who sees me,' for she said, 'I have now seen the One who sees me'" (Genesis 16:13).

That name she calls God is *El Roi*, and in Hebrew it literally means "The God who sees me."[5] Hagar is declaring, "God sees me, and I see Him." Doesn't that remind you of sweet Lucy? Locking gazes with God has the power to reverse a curse we have believed because suddenly we understand that His care for us is deeply personal. He not only knows our name, but He is willing to chase us down and reveal His name to us in an extraordinary way. I love this note of the encounter, which says, "That is why the well was called Beer Lahai Roi; it is still there, between Kadesh and Bered" (Genesis 16:14). Not only did she give God a name (the only person in the Old Testament to do this), but before she goes back to her mistress Sarai, she named the place where she encountered the God who saw her. "Beer-lahai-roi means 'the well of the living one who sees me.'"[6] Maybe she did that so others who wandered in their own wilderness would have a little bit of hope when the view in their mirror was dark and obscure. She was reaching forward for others and pulling them along to the bigger story.

Another Well in Another Time and Place

Now you might be thinking that the story has the feel of an old blockbuster movie with Charlton Heston and is a little unrelatable. I get it. But do you know that the Bible tells us that Jesus Christ is the same yesterday, today, and forever? (see Hebrews 13:8) The God of the Old Testament shows up in the New Testament with the same attributes. Jesus demonstrated that He saw people too, and He wasn't afraid to take a detour off the beaten path to encounter another woman who was hiding at a well:

> Now he had to go through Samaria. So he came to a town in Samaria called Sychar, near the plot of ground Jacob had given to his son Joseph. Jacob's well was there, and Jesus, tired as he was from the journey, sat down by the well. It was about noon. When a Samaritan woman came to draw water, Jesus said to her, "Will you give me a drink?"
>
> John 4:4–7

In this story from John 4, you can read the longest conversation recorded in the Bible between Jesus and a person. Let me pause here and say that any conversation we have in Scripture between Jesus and a person is a gift. But in a time when women and girls were not having a historical cultural moment, this moment with Jesus and a foreign woman at a well is extraordinary. Jesus talks to her about many things, including history and the well itself. He goes on to say:

> Everyone who drinks this water will be thirsty again, but whoever drinks the water I give them will never thirst. Indeed, the water I give them will become in them a spring of water welling up to eternal life.
>
> John 4:13–14

Suddenly He has her attention, because water in the Middle East is everything. She quickly assumes this special water will solve all her immediate problems. Her own view of her life involves the public ridicule she has faced after five failed marriages. Jesus doesn't shy away from her story when tells her, "Go, call your husband and come back" (John 4:16). Jesus, full of grace and truth, isn't trying to heap shame upon her. He is simply saying, *I am the God who sees you*. Listen, that is powerful when you don't want to be seen and you are fetching water during the hottest part of the day because the whispers of others feel like fireballs of condemnation. Being seen with grace is better than water in the desert. It is a spring of water that does not fail—ever.

My favorite part of this story is that she tests the waters herself when she says, "'I know that Messiah' (called Christ) 'is coming. When he comes, he will explain everything to us'" (John 4:25). And without hesitation He declares, "I, the one speaking to you—I am he" (John 4:26).

At a well called Beer-lahai-roi, the living one sees a broken-down woman, and at Jacob's well, a broken-down woman sees the living one. Jesus not only sees her, He lets her in on a secret He has yet to tell anyone else up until this point: "I Am has come." Just like He said He would. And He came *to her and for her*. Friend, Jesus pursues the hearts of His daughters, and it doesn't matter if we are living in a foreign land, running away from a difficult circumstance, or hiding in the middle of our broken-down life. Jesus comes for us too. This reminds me of Psalm 139:7–10:

> Where can I go from your Spirit?
> Where can I flee from your presence?
> If I go up to the heavens, you are there;
> if I make my bed in the depths, you are there.
> If I rise on the wings of the dawn,

if I settle on the far side of the sea,
even there your hand will guide me,
your right hand will hold me fast.

With this idea in mind, the Victorian era poet Francis Thompson coined the term "Hound of Heaven" to describe how God pursues with relentless determination.[7] At His heart, God is determined to pursue those who belong to Him with a passion that can't be thwarted, even by our own wrong choices or circumstances. He is with us. He guides us. He holds us fast. And most importantly, He sees us no matter what.

Praying for Your Teen Girl

I don't know about you, but these stories give me hope—amid the hard data that girls today are struggling—to put one foot in front of the other. I need a reminder that Jesus isn't unaware and that I can partner with Him and pray for my teen girl's heart. Do you know that these two women experienced radical change in their lives when they met the Lord in the middle of their mess? In the heartbeat of a moment, that dark mirror blazed bright, and they saw El Roi pursuing their hearts with love. And that made all the difference in the world.

I want that kind of love story for my teen girls. I want to sing it over their hearts louder than a stadium full of Swifties. I want them to know without a shadow of a doubt that they are seen, and their heart is worth pursuing. It is the most life-changing love of all.

This is how much God loved the world: He gave his Son, his one and only Son. And this is why: so that no one need be destroyed; by believing in him, anyone can have a whole and lasting life.

John 3:16 MSG

So, the next time you get a chance to hold your girl in a hug or merely with your prayers, whisper over her the words you can be sure our Father in heaven loves to respond to because they are His words of truth. Pray, "Lord, pursue her heart." You can even slip her name in that verse and say, "This is how much God loves you (Emma, Abigail, Caroline, and Alison . . .). He gave His Son so you don't need to be destroyed, and when you believe in Him, you can have a life that is whole and everlasting. All because He loves you."

"LORD, PURSUE HER HEART" PRAYERS

Philippians 1:6—"Being confident of this, that he who began a good work in you will carry it on to completion until the day of Christ Jesus."

> **PRAYER:** Father, thank you that I can be certain you have started a good work in _____ . I pray you will keep working in her life and that she will be flourishing on the day Jesus returns to redeem the world. In Jesus' name, Amen.

Ephesians 1:3–4—"Praise be to the God and Father of our Lord Jesus Christ, who has blessed us in the heavenly realms with every spiritual blessing in Christ. For he chose us in him before the creation of the world to be holy and blameless in his sight."

> **PRAYER:** Father, I praise you for blessing _____ with every spiritual blessing in Christ. She was chosen and set apart by you before the world began to live a holy and blameless life. You see her completely free of sin because of Jesus. May she honor you for these abundant blessings. In Jesus' name, Amen.

Psalm 139:17—"How precious to me are your thoughts, God! How vast is the sum of them!"

> **PRAYER:** Father, you not only know _____ , but you think of her constantly. I pray that she will hold on to the sweet admiration you have for her and treasure it in her heart. In Jesus' name, Amen.

Jeremiah 31:3—"The LORD appeared to us in the past, saying: 'I have loved you with an everlasting love; I have drawn you with unfailing kindness.'"

> **PRAYER:** Father, thank you that your love for _____ never stops. I pray you will draw her close with your faithful lovingkindness. In Jesus' name, Amen.

Isaiah 54:10—"'Though the mountains be shaken and the hills be removed, yet my unfailing love for you will not be shaken nor my covenant of peace be removed,' says the LORD, who has compassion on you."

> **PRAYER:** Father, your love for _____ does not walk away, it never fails, and it can't be removed. I pray your unshakable love and your promise of peace will permeate her entire life.

John 3:16—"For God so loved the world that he gave his one and only Son, that whoever believes in him shall not perish but have eternal life."

> **PRAYER:** Father, thank you that you so loved _____ that you gave her your one and only Son. I pray she will trust in you so that she will not lose her life but instead have one that is whole and everlasting. In Jesus' name, Amen.

Romans 8:31—"What, then, shall we say in response to these things? If God is for us, who can be against us?"

> **PRAYER:** Father, thank you that you are for _____.
> Since you are on her side, she doesn't have to be afraid
> because nothing is ever impossible with you on her side.
> Show her in big and small ways that you are for her. In Jesus'
> name, Amen.

1 John 4:9–11—"This is how God showed his love among us: He sent his one and only Son into the world that we might live through him. This is love: not that we loved God, but that he loved us and sent his Son as an atoning sacrifice for our sins. Dear friends, since God so loved us, we also ought to love one another."

> **PRAYER:** Father, you showed your love to _____ by
> sending Jesus into the world so that she might live through
> Him. May she experience this real love that comes from you
> and through Christ, who is the perfect sacrifice for her sins.
> Let this love be what motivates her to love those around her
> at home, school, and church. In Jesus' name, Amen.

Galatians 2:20—"I have been crucified with Christ and I no longer live, but Christ lives in me. The life I now live in the body, I live by faith in the Son of God, who loved me and gave himself for me."

> **PRAYER:** Father, I pray that _____ will be completely
> identified with you to the point that she isn't living for herself
> anymore, but for you. I pray she will live a beautiful life of com-
> plete trust in Christ, who not only loved her but sacrificed His
> life for her. In Jesus' name, Amen.

1 John 3:1—"See what great love the Father has lavished on us, that we should be called children of God! And that is what we are! The reason the world does not know us is that it did not know him."

PRAYER: Father, I pray _____ will consider the incredible love you have shown her by calling her your daughter. May she be rooted in this love and let it soften the edges of any rejection she may encounter because of how it flows in and through her life. In Jesus' name, Amen.

PRAYERS AND NOTES

4

LORD, MAY SHE SEEK WHAT IS TRUE

As we pore over the Word, the Holy Spirit will help us discern truth from lies. A right understanding of Scripture leads to a life of obedience that looks radically different from the world around us.[1]

Mary Wiley

I am the worst at games. I think it is somehow related to my lack of competitive spirit. I'd rather cheer for you than beat you to the finish line. However, give me a game of words like *2 Truths and a Lie* and I might come out the victor. Can you spot the lie?

I sang at my local Walmart in front of the women's department.

My hometown was once called Lick Skillet.

I have a sister.

You have a distinct advantage in this game if you've known me for more than five minutes or you happen to have grown up with me. For example, you'd know that I grew up in a small town in Southern Indiana called North Vernon that was once named *Lick Skillet*. You would also know my only sibling is my older brother named Trent. You would probably remember that my grandfather owned a popular women's and children's department store called *Stoners Fashions*, which I never sang at, *but I did sing once at Walmart*. To sort truth from lies, you obviously need to know something about me. You need to know my history, my character, and my name. All of these facts point to the truth of who I am, how I live my life, and what decisions I am likely to make.

The same applies for our teen girls. They don't necessarily need to know about *me* (unless they happen to be one of the teen girls living in my house). They need to know the truth about God, His character, and His name. Knowing and seeking truth about God will inform who they are in light of that truth. It will instruct them on how to live their lives and then give them wisdom to make decisions that will be for their own personal good and His ultimate glory.

My friend Judy is a therapist and school counselor. She is also the ad hoc counselor of our group of college friends that I still have almost daily contact with via the Marco Polo app on our phones. Among the eight of us, we have fourteen girls, and a few are still teenagers. So, when I asked her about helping teen girls seek what is true, she spoke, and all of us leaned in to listen. She gave permission to share what she said here:

I'm constantly trying to get teen girls to question their thoughts, telling them, *Just because you have a thought doesn't mean that it is true.* And also, a lot of their thoughts come from mean comments that were made at some point in their lives—like a brother or a bully. It's like they grab on to a thought and believe it as truth. Normally it is far from the truth (about them). On the other hand, they could have heard a bunch of truth from their parents about how beautiful they are and how they have worth and value. But one mean comment that is made sticks with them. I see this more with girls than boys. My goal as a counselor is to loosen their thoughts to even give them the possibility to think the thought may not be true. That is the first step to recognize what they are saying about themselves. And then she can question it. Even better, when I work with kids who are Christians, their identity in Christ and what God has to say about who they are makes a big difference.

I was especially intrigued by her perspective that for teen girls, lies and untruth tend to "stick with them." In order to get to the root of what they are believing, we need to loosen their thoughts and give them the possibility that what they are thinking may not be true at all. At the same time, a teen girl who knows and understands her identity in Christ and what God says about her will be able to spot those lies more quickly. As you can imagine, this is not neutral territory. The enemy of our souls has been attempting to take this ground from young women since the garden. His aim is pretty decent too. So get ready, this prayer may seem more like warfare.

Did God Really Say?

> Now the serpent was more crafty than any of the wild animals the LORD God had made. He said to the woman, "Did God really say, 'You must not eat from any tree in the garden'?"
>
> Genesis 3:1

Do you want a tale truly as old as time? This one fits the narrative. It is found in the book of beginnings, Genesis, which was passed down from generation to generation. It is a critical part of God's story and His relationship to the world and humanity.

God created and established an order that He communicated to His first two children, Adam and Eve. Apparently, the serpent knew this, and he used it to his advantage. He was craftier than others like him. And by crafty I'm not saying he was adept at making macramé plant hangers or painting pottery. His craftiness took the form of a subtle slyness that he used to cast doubt on what God had said and how His children were able to remember and apply His words. Notice that the serpent didn't deny that God had spoken. He didn't even debate that God was the creator and judge of the world. What he poked at and began to disassemble in plain sight was *what* God said: *Are you sure that is what He actually said?*

> The woman said to the serpent, "We may eat fruit from the trees in the garden, but God did say, 'You must not eat fruit from the tree that is in the middle of the garden, and you must not touch it, or you will die.'"
>
> Genesis 3:2–3

Eve, without missing a beat, parroted to the serpent the information he was after. Let's set aside the horror we all feel about Eve talking to the serpent as if that is normal (which apparently it was for her, which also begs more questions). She spoke some truth. But she didn't quite get it right. So, what did God really say? Genesis 2:16–17 gives us the truth of what God said:

> And the LORD God commanded the man, "You are free to eat from any tree in the garden; but you must not eat from the tree of the knowledge of good and evil, for when you eat from it you will certainly die."

Do you see the subtle difference? Eve's version said, "you must not touch it, or you will die." God's truth said, "you must

not eat from the tree . . . for when you eat from it you will certainly die." God didn't say, "Don't touch it." He said, "Don't
eat from it." It may not seem like a big deal. I misquote what
other people say all the time. But this wasn't just anyone. This
was God. And this was part of His instruction on how they were
to live and flourish in the Garden. It was for their ultimate joy
and protection. The sneaky serpent had his crack to enter and
used it expertly to swing wide open the door of doubt for Eve.

> "You will not certainly die," the serpent said to the woman. "For
> God knows that when you eat from it your eyes will be opened,
> and you will be like God, knowing good and evil."
>
> Genesis 3:4–5

Oh come on. You won't die. That's harsh. God is just holding
out on you because He doesn't want you to be like Him.

> When the woman saw that the fruit of the tree was good for food
> and pleasing to the eye, and also desirable for gaining wisdom,
> she took some and ate it. She also gave some to her husband,
> who was with her, and he ate it. Then the eyes of both of them
> were opened, and they realized they were naked; so they sewed
> fig leaves together and made coverings for themselves.
>
> Genesis 3:6–7

Don't miss this. She believed a subtle tweak of the truth. She
listened to the serpent more than what God said. She created
her own version of the truth (with more than a fair amount
of leading from the serpent), and she took action because she
wanted wisdom on her own terms. The result was not what she
sought. It was an eye-opening awareness that was more than she
bargained for—both for her and Adam. Who, by the way, was
just as involved as Eve was because he knew what God said, was

with her as she was having the conversation with the serpent, and didn't say a word. Adam willingly ate too and suffered devastating consequences as well. Genesis 3 goes on to tell us that after they realized they were naked and vulnerable, they quickly covered their bodies and hid from their creator—God—who was already pursuing their sin-soaked hearts. He found them buried in shame and set in holy motion the eternal plan to save them. As it turned out, it would require a once-for-all death on another tree thousands of years later by His Son, Jesus.

You may wonder what the story of Adam and Eve in the garden has to do with your teen girl. I believe it has everything to do with her. The enemy of our girls (and our own souls) does not have any new tricks up his slimy sleeves. He is infamous for taking a bit of truth and mixing it with a sweet and subtle lie that appeals to our own selfish desires. He mixes these half-truths up and spits them back out at breakneck speed before we can untangle the truth from the deception. And very often we buy them as an acceptable form of the truth. Which, of course, is not the truth at all. Lies stick because they are appealing and believable. Our teen girls will be delightfully easy targets for the enemy until they realize they were made for the whole truth of God's Word.

Jesus Prays and So Can We

This is a book about praying for teen girls. Any time I can point to an actual prayer in Scripture we can grab on to, it is a no-brainer. Did you know there are over 650 prayers in the Bible?[2] I'm pretty sure more than a few of those would be perfect for this book, and I will be sure to include them. But when I can show you some red-letter words of Jesus about prayer, that is even better, don't you think? Jesus prayed a lot in His three years of public ministry. There are several places where the writers of the Gospels tell us Jesus slipped away to pray. He was asked by His disciples to teach them how to pray, and in Luke 11:1–4 Jesus was happy to fill in the gaps for them on what God-honoring prayer looks like. In addition to that passage, there are at least twenty-four other places in the Bible that record the prayers of Jesus.[3]

My favorite prayer of Jesus is found in John 17 and occurred on the night He was arrested, the day before He was crucified. Hours before He would die, He prayed for His disciples, and He prayed for our teen girls. He prayed for you and me too. The prayer is twenty-six verses long, and it is beautiful. I want to encourage you to study it. The verses I want to point out to you here are John 17:13–19 (emphasis added):

> I am coming to you now, but I say these things while I am still in the world, so that they may have the full measure of my joy within them. I have given them your word and the world has hated them, for they are not of the world any more than I am of the world. My prayer is not that you take them out of the world but that you protect them from the evil one. They are not of the world, even as I am not of it. *Sanctify them by the truth; your word is truth.* As you sent me into the world, I have sent them into the world. For them I sanctify myself, that they too may be truly sanctified.

Jesus knows this world. He created it and lived in it. He knows the key to our own flourishing is God's Word embedded in our hearts. He prayed for our protection from the evil one (aka the serpent) and that we would be *sanctified* by truth. Just in case you haven't used the word *sanctified* on an Instagram post lately, it means "to separate, set apart or appoint to a holy, sacred or religious use."[4] Jesus wanted the truth found only in God's Word to set us apart and make us radically different from the world around us. The Word makes our teen girls distinctive. It makes them more like Jesus. And in the end, the world probably won't celebrate them. At the very least, there will be times when others won't understand them and may even despise or hate them. Jesus said it. We can bank on it.

When It Feels Like Too Much

Now, this may feel heavy. I get it. I'm a mom of teen girls and also doing my best to be a woman of the Word who knows how to wield the weapon of the Word well. Those sticky lies I mentioned earlier will lead our girls (and us) to being easy targets for the enemy to tempt us to sin (1 Peter 5:8–10). But is this a no-win situation? Absolutely not. This is simply the truth of what we are fighting for on our knees for our teen girls. It is a messy world. Truth that is accepted apart from God's Word is relative. Everyone gets to decide on their own version of it for their own little manufactured worlds. You do you. I do me. We all get to do what we think and believe is true. Guess where that has landed our girls? If you read chapter 1 already, you know the answer to that question. And you probably knew that already.

I don't want to simply give you sweet prayers that sound like the songs I sang as a child about the birds that sing and the food we eat. Those are all good for drifting off to sleep and have their place. Yet I can't help but notice that when Jesus was moments from the cross, He didn't mince words. He wasn't desperate, but He did pray for us to be protected by the Word and set apart in truth. He asked God to keep us, and He knew that this was the only way.

I know some of you are heartbroken over the current situation your teen girl finds herself in these days because she is wandering far from the truth. I've read your Facebook posts and emails. I've seen the tears in your eyes as you tell me that you are at the end of your rope. You don't know what to do or what to tell her. You don't need a platitude and a pat on the hand. You might want me to tell you it will be okay, and I would say that as I hug you if I could. But what you really need is a plan that will help you get in the fight for and alongside your teen girl.

Jesus said, "If you hold to my teaching, you are really my disciples. Then you will know the truth, and the truth will set you free" (John 8:31–32). This prayer, that our teen girls will seek what is true, is a prayer for them to be anchored in the Word, to live with discernment, and to walk obediently in truth that will truly set them free.

You aren't desperate, my friend. You have solid, anchoring hope because you have access to God through prayer. He has invited us to approach Him boldly and make our requests (see Hebrews 4:16). Can you imagine praying this prayer with the authority of God's Word? Can you see your teen girl truly free? She won't be hiding in sin-soaked shame anymore. She won't need to play games of lies and truth. She will find her great reward in the One who is the way, truth, and life. And His words will be sweeter than honey and her great reward.

Amen. Let it be so.

"LORD, MAY SHE SEEK WHAT IS TRUE" PRAYERS

Colossians 3:1–2—"Since, then, you have been raised with Christ, set your hearts on things above, where Christ is, seated at the right hand of God. Set your minds on things above, not on earthly things."

PRAYER: Father, I pray that _____ will give her heart to the heavenly things that matter to you, not earthly things that only have temporal value. May she also set her mind continually on what is above and truly see things from your perspective. In Jesus' name, Amen.

James 1:5—"If any of you lacks wisdom, you should ask God, who gives generously to all without finding fault, and it will be given to you."

PRAYER: Father, I pray that if _____ doesn't know what to do, she will pray and ask you for help. May she remember that you are a good father who gives generously without making us feel foolish for asking. In Jesus' name, Amen.

Psalm 86:11—"Teach me your way, LORD, that I may rely on your faithfulness; give me an undivided heart, that I may fear your name."

PRAYER: Father, teach _____ your way so she may walk and live in truth. There are so many distractions in this world; I pray she will have an undivided heart that will be in awe of your great name. In Jesus' name, Amen.

Psalm 111:10—"The fear of the LORD is the beginning of wisdom; all who follow his precepts have good understanding. To him belongs eternal praise."

PRAYER: Father, having respect for you is essential for growing in wisdom. I pray that _____ will follow your ways and have a teachable heart while always worshiping you in reverent awe. In Jesus' name, Amen.

John 17:17–19—"Sanctify them by the truth; your word is truth. As you sent me into the world, I have sent them into the world. For them I sanctify myself, that they too may be truly sanctified."

PRAYER: Father, you have set _____ apart for your purpose by the truth of your Word. I pray you will completely immerse her in your truth so she will understand that she has everything she needs to do your will. Thank you that you have made _____ holy, separated her from the world, and sent her to be your witness. In Jesus' name, Amen.

3 John 1:4—"I have no greater joy than to hear that my children are walking in the truth."

PRAYER: Father, I pray that _____ will diligently follow the way of truth every single day of her life. In Jesus' name, Amen.

2 Corinthians 10:5—"We demolish arguments and every pretension that sets itself up against the knowledge of God, and we take captive every thought to make it obedient to Christ."

PRAYER: Father, I pray that _____ will understand that the battle she is facing is spiritual at every level. May she be able to recognize, capture, and tear down every lie contrary to the knowledge of God. Help _____ to know it is the power of the gospel that allows her to take those thoughts and surrender them to the Lordship of Christ in her life. In Jesus' name, Amen.

Ephesians 5:15–17—"Be very careful, then, how you live— not as unwise but as wise, making the most of every opportunity, because the days are evil. Therefore do not be foolish, but understand what the Lord's will is."

PRAYER: Father, I pray that _____ will not waste precious time but will realize the responsibility she has to live

carefully and not tolerate evil of any kind. Help _____
to have a discerning spirit and to follow hard after you. In Jesus'
name, Amen.

Romans 1:16—"For I am not ashamed of the gospel, because
it is the power of God that brings salvation to everyone who
believes: first to the Jew, then to the Gentile."

> **PRAYER:** Father, may _____ not be ashamed of the good
> news of Jesus Christ because it has the dynamic power to bring
> salvation to everyone who believes. In Jesus' name, Amen.

1 Thessalonians 1:5—"Because our gospel came to you not
simply with words but also with power, with the Holy Spirit
and deep conviction. You know how we lived among you for
your sake."

> **PRAYER:** Father, it is my prayer that the gospel would come not
> only in words for _____ but also with life-changing
> power from the Holy Spirit. May she have the complete cer-
> tainty that comes with a transformed life. In Jesus' name, Amen.

PRAYERS AND NOTES

5

LORD, MAKE HER STRONG

The world cannot fathom strength proceeding from weakness, gain proceeding from loss, or power from meekness. [1]

Elisabeth Elliot

"No help, Mommy. I can do it."

She was a tiny and determined two-year-old who suddenly didn't need me anymore. Or so she declared. After so many years of being her mom, it still makes me smile to think of the fierce determination in her bright blue eyes. Truthfully, after waving off my offer of help, she more than confidently proceeded to do the thing in question without so much as a casual glance my way for assistance. She did, however, throw up her hands in the air and squeal "Ta-da!" rather triumphantly. Every. Single. Time.

But today, she isn't little anymore. And the things she needs to do are often so overwhelming I couldn't begin to help her even if I wanted to. It will take more than me and my motherly advice to make it in this world. She will need strength that comes from a completely different source. And part of the way God seems to answer this prayer is for her to realize that it isn't her strength but His, and it is forged in the furnace of hardships we wouldn't wish on our worst enemy, let alone on our teen girls.

Moving from "Em-Powered" to "Powered Within"

Remember in a previous chapter when I mentioned that girls were having a cultural moment? Girl power is a hot topic, and if you try to argue any differently in the public square you are seen as a narrow-minded person. When I looked up the word *empower* in the dictionary, this is what I found:

> . . . to give official authority or legal power to; enable; to promote the self-actualization or influence of; "The American women's movement has been inspiring and *empowering* women for nearly 20 years . . ."—Ron Hansen[2]

Do you want your teen girl to be empowered? Look no further than the dictionary to be inspired. But does this push toward liberation give our girls a real sense of power? Do teen girls feel that way today? Truly? I asked my teen daughters recently, "Do you think teen girls feel strong?" And they both said without missing a beat, "Absolutely not. I think they feel the opposite." So, who do you believe?

Certainly, by the world's standard for empowerment, the teen girls we are driven to our knees to pray for are already empowered. They have clean water, housing, and access to education that will help them achieve their dreams. These are all amazing things we should of course be grateful for, especially if you look at statistics worldwide of girls at risk. But I'm talking about girls who should feel strong but don't. Maybe that is because the world's definition of empowerment only lasts as long as you are succeeding or as long as you have influence that others crave on social media. The truth is that this type of power and influence is fleeting and not at all what we want for our teen girls. My friend Jeannie Cunnion says it like this:

> As Christians, we are set free from striving to be the superheroes of our stories! We are liberated from relying on our own inner strength, which in reality isn't all that impressive, but it is super exhausting. Can we just admit that together? Our inner strength—apart from God's inner strengthening—isn't much to brag about. But there's a good reason for that. God didn't design us to do *anything* apart from His Spirit. So if we buy in to the messaging that we can mantra up whatever it is that we need to navigate the struggles of this life, we forego witnessing what's only possible with the Spirit. What a travesty that would be.[3]

God didn't design our teen girls to be strong—or empowered—on their own. We are all designed to be powered within by nothing less than His Holy Spirit. The good news is that this type of power is not only life-changing, it is endless. Jesus told His followers, "But very truly I tell you, it is for your good that I am going away. Unless I go away, the Advocate will not come to you; but if I go, I will send him to you" (John 16:7).

The Advocate Jesus is referring to is the Holy Spirit, who acts as our counselor, friend, comforter, intercessor, and strengthener. And Jesus knew that He was exactly who we would need on our good and hard days.

The world will keep pushing the message that our girls are liberated when they are free to live as they please without the constrictions of their gender. But we know a better way. And while it can be a tough lesson to watch our girls learn, it is even more exhausting (as Jeannie says) to let them be convinced they are superheroes who don't need anyone or anything to make it in everyday life. On the other hand, God's way may seem upside-down, especially when you read verses like this:

> But he said to me, "My grace is sufficient for you, for my power is made perfect in weakness." Therefore I will boast all the more gladly about my weaknesses, so that Christ's power may rest on me. That is why, for Christ's sake, I delight in weaknesses, in insults, in hardships, in persecutions, in difficulties. For when I am weak, then I am strong.
>
> 2 Corinthians 12:9–10

Can we honestly pray for our girls to be strong while understanding all too well that God often perfects His strength in them when they come to the end of themselves? Oh, friend, we may not want to, but we must get out of the way and pray that very prayer.

God the Lord Is My Strength

Nobody likes to feel weak. I don't know why, but women (especially) seem to spend an inordinate amount of time pretending to have it all together. Let me be one-hundred-percent truthful here and say without a doubt I have powered through, gritted my teeth, and lived a life of self-sufficiency for years in front of my four girls. It wasn't until our lives fell apart several years ago during a long season of loss, illness, and trauma that I had to let go of that mirage of my own making. I could no longer figure it out, dig deep, or even come up with answers to their simple questions about what we were going to do tomorrow. But what I could do was point them to God, pray in the name of Jesus, and ask the Holy Spirit to strengthen them in a way that I never could.

During that time in our lives, I lived wholeheartedly in a passage of Scripture from the book of Habakkuk. It says:

> Though the fig tree does not bud
>   and there are no grapes on the vines,
> though the olive crop fails
>   and the fields produce no food,
> though there are no sheep in the pen
>   and no cattle in the stalls,
> yet I will rejoice in the Lord,
>   I will be joyful in God my Savior.
>
> Habakkuk 3:17–18

These verses were a signpost for me to remember that no matter what our circumstances held, my response was to look to God. I did this somewhat imperfectly in front of my girls, but the phrase "Even if . . . I still will" became so engraved on my heart that I put it on a T-shirt and my favorite coffee mug and was not ashamed to say that I was completely fresh out of amazing.

But this year, amid His ongoing rebuilding of our lives, God pointed me to the next verse in this chapter. It says:

> The Sovereign Lord is my strength;
>   he makes my feet like the feet of a deer,
>   he enables me to tread on the heights.
>
> Habakkuk 3:19

In the original language the verse calls God "Jehovah Adonai." This is a declaration of Habakkuk's hard-fought faith—through loss, war, famine, and failure. He wasn't relying on his strength but finally at rest in God's. Kenneth L. Barker explains, "The names emphasize the power and majesty of

God. Habakkuk used the strongest names for God available."⁴
The use of *Lord* also shows the personal nature of the name.
Habakkuk knew God as both powerful *and* personal because
of all he had gone through. In addition, the word for *strength*
can translate into "army."⁵ I can't tell you how many times in
the past few months I have said repeatedly, "God the Lord is
my army." When I have felt tired, overwhelmed, out of ideas,
beyond my capabilities, and alone, I have been able to finally
lean into the meaning of this prayer.

> God the Lord is my strength.
> He makes my feet steady in uncertain places.
> He allows me to walk in victory because He has a
> purpose and a plan.

Last week, I sat in my pastor's office, talking about various
things. Toward the end of our time together he said to me, "I
knew your family was faithful, but I didn't know who you really
were until I watched you walk through the past few years with
your family. That showed me who you really are in the Lord. It
was in your weakness that God's power was evident." It's true;
the mirage I had maintained of my own strength was shattered
under the weight of our trials. And to think, not only my pastor
but also my girls have had a front-row seat to my undoing. My
pride would tell you I'm embarrassed. But honestly, I've never
been more grateful that my girls know the truth.

When She Is Facing Something Bigger Than She Is

It is one thing for me to feel weak and be seen as weak in front
of my girls. That is hard enough. But I'm not sure I've ever felt
more helpless than watching my girls go through their own
hardships that carved out space for God's Spirit to dwell in

a more significant way because they were weak and in such need of Him. I wanted to rush in, provide the power, and fix the problem. Sometimes a mom can and should do that very thing—especially when our girls are little. But not always. And not perfectly.

My girls all have faced something bigger than themselves. They've also witnessed miracles and provision that they otherwise would not have experienced had they been spared from such hardships. If I had been the one calling the shots, I can tell you with no uncertainty that I would have said, "No, this is not happening in their lives." I would have pushed back the waves that threatened to overwhelm them while they were clinging to a tiny life raft for dear life. I would have held back the storm because it wasn't fair for such young girls to be exposed to so much in a short amount of time. And in the process, I would have made life in that season easier. I would have given them the cheap strength knock-off this world offers instead of the real thing. They might have felt empowered, but they wouldn't have been in-powered.

My daughter Caroline was diagnosed with an autoimmune disease well before she was in her teen years. I remember sitting beside her bed in the hospital when we didn't know what was happening. I was terrified to close my eyes for fear she might slip away from me in the night. In my fear, I clung to her until the Lord reminded me that He loved her even more than I did, and I could trust the work He was doing in and through her life. I didn't like it, but I surrendered her to Him that morning.

Since that day, I've witnessed her ever-growing faith as she has experienced medical tests and treatments that I'm not sure many adults could handle. We are often reminded that this isn't the story we would have chosen, but God has been faithful and present every step of the way. One time when we were driving to and from one of her many procedures, I asked her,

"You've had to go through a lot over the past few years. What would you want other people to know about it?" She paused, and thoughtfully said, "Mom, before I got sick I didn't really think much about God because I didn't need Him. But since I've been sick, I have thought about God and talked to Him every day, and that is not a bad thing."

No, it isn't a bad thing at all. It is a deep thing, and it is only forged in the fire of a life lived between the now and not yet. Our girls live in a world that wants them to be strong on their own but that falls dreadfully short of God's answer. At the same time, the world will absolutely chew her up and spit her back out when her own strength falls short (as it inevitably will). Let's be brave enough to ask Him for His strength to be ever growing in our own lives and the lives of our teen girls. It is so much better. No matter the cost.

"LORD, MAKE HER STRONG" PRAYERS

Habakkuk 3:19—"The Sovereign LORD is my strength; he makes my feet like the feet of a deer, he enables me to tread on the heights."

> **PRAYER:** Father, I pray that _____ will know you as Jehovah Adonai (God the Lord), who is like a powerful army on her behalf. May she rest completely in your ability to help her take courageous and confident steps during challenging times. In Jesus' name, Amen.

Ephesians 5:18–19—"Do not get drunk on wine, which leads to debauchery. Instead, be filled with the Spirit, speaking to one another with psalms, hymns, and songs from the Spirit. Sing and make music from your heart to the Lord."

PRAYER: Father, the world will try to tempt _____ to take her fill of things that don't truly satisfy. I pray instead that she will be filled to the overflow with your Spirit and that it will influence her to encourage others and offer praise deep within her heart always and forever to you. In Jesus' name, Amen.

John 16:7—"But very truly I tell you, it is for your good that I am going away. Unless I go away, the Advocate will not come to you; but if I go, I will send him to you."

PRAYER: Father, thank you that when Jesus went to heaven He sent the Holy Spirit as a helper for _____. I pray that she will enjoy close fellowship with you as her comforter, advocate, intercessor, and the one who strengthens her every day. In Jesus' name, Amen.

Hebrews 13:5—"God has said, 'Never will I leave you; never will I forsake you.'"

PRAYER: Father, may _____ understand that because you said it she can believe it. There will never be any circumstance when you will walk away from her. I pray that she will remember that she is not helpless because you will never fail her. In Jesus' name, Amen.

1 Corinthians 2:12—"What we have received is not the spirit of the world, but the Spirit who is from God, so that we may understand what God has freely given us."

PRAYER: Father, it is a marvelous truth that you have given _____ your Spirit. She doesn't have to guess or rely on the wisdom of the world because she has been freely given the grace of God. I pray she will know and understand this wonderful gift you have given her. In Jesus' name, Amen.

Joshua 1:9—"Have I not commanded you? Be strong and courageous. Do not be afraid; do not be discouraged, for the Lord your God will be with you wherever you go."

PRAYER: Father, when _____ remembers that you are with her wherever she goes, she doesn't have to be fearful or discouraged. I pray that instead she will take bold and strong steps of faith because with you she can banish fear and erase any doubts. In Jesus' name, Amen.

Philippians 4:13—"I can do all this through him who gives me strength."

PRAYER: Father, I pray that _____ will believe that if you have called her to do something, she is equal to the task because of your sufficient strength. May she experience not only that inner strength but your confident peace as well. In Jesus' name, Amen.

2 Corinthians 12:9–10—"But he said to me, 'My grace is sufficient for you, for my power is made perfect in weakness.' Therefore I will boast all the more gladly about my weaknesses, so that Christ's power may rest on me. That is why, for Christ's sake, I delight in weaknesses, in insults, in hardships, in persecutions, in difficulties. For when I am weak, then I am strong."

PRAYER: Father, your grace is enough for _____ and always available to her. It shows up powerfully in her weakness so that she can be a display of your strength to others. May she even take delight when she faces hard days and difficult people because less of her means more of you. In Jesus' name, Amen.

Psalm 73:26—"My flesh and my heart may fail, but God is the strength of my heart and my portion forever."

PRAYER: Father, I know there will be times when _____ feels like she is completely at the end of herself. I pray that on those days she will remember you are her rock and that you never run out of strength. In Jesus' name, Amen.

Nehemiah 8:10—". . . for the joy of the LORD is your strength."

PRAYER: Father, I pray that _____ will experience your soul-invigorating joy today. Joy is not like happiness, which changes with circumstances. True, deep-down joy from you acts as a protection over her life, because where you dwell you strengthen and restore. In Jesus' name, Amen.

6

LORD, KEEP HER SOFT

He knows me fully—every thought and every intention, every perception and every judgment, every response to the world around me, no personality test required. . . . Apprehending with complete accuracy the best and the worst of me, he is neither impressed nor horrified. He accepts me as I am because of Christ.[1]

Jen Wilkin

I am not a fan of stereotypes and clichés. Here are a few I have battled over the years:

- Cheerleaders are popular and mean.
- Homeschool moms only wear denim jumpers.
- Writers are grammar geeks.

Growing up, I wanted to be a cheerleader for as long as I could remember. I didn't aspire to it because I thought it would gain me access to the popular crowd at school (it didn't, by the way). I truly wanted to be a cheerleader because I loved cheering for my team. I loved galvanizing the crowd. I loved talking. Okay, that might be part of the stereotype.

Similarly, when my family decided to begin the homeschooling journey almost twenty years ago, I was well beyond the denim jumper phase that was actually popular in the 1990s. I confess I did own one during that time and borrowed a much cuter one from my college roommate. But I don't think I've worn one since that unfortunate fashion trend ended. You are most likely to find me in a faded pair of jeans and a graphic T-shirt when I am struggling through my fifth round of Algebra.

And before you think my grammar could win any award or impress my high school English teacher, Mrs. Thill, you need only to email my editors. Yes, that is plural for a reason. I do happen to have a strong love of words, dictionaries, and writing sentences. But anyone who is tasked with reading my first draft will tell you grammar is not my gift (insert smile here from my very qualified and gifted line editors who just highlighted this sentence and took a drink of their coffee in salute). They know the truth and have been sworn to secrecy.

Stereotypes about teenage girls are prevalent. The media will tell you they are lazy, uncommunicative with parents, and don't care about anyone but themselves. You probably see these generalizations pop up as memes in social media as well as from many of your friends. One of my favorites has to do with how many dishes teens have in their bedrooms. Y'all, I haven't seen my favorite coffee cup in months. I'm pretty sure it is buried under so much dirty laundry in my daughter's room I wouldn't want it back if I could have it sterilized and presented to me on a silver tray with my morning coffee.

You smile because that part is true. Sometimes stereotypes have threads of truth in them as well, which is why we are prone to hold to them and prepare ourselves for the inevitable. I truly want to tread carefully here because after raising four teen girls, I can tell you that some commonly held beliefs about teen girls are fairly accurate. When you find yourself in the middle of a discussion and your teen girl says or does something you didn't see coming, it hits you: *Oh, there it is. She is a teenager after all.* But at the same time, I don't want to box your teen girl into behavior that is universally expected just because she is between the ages of eleven and twenty. Your girl is a person, and she may or may not behave in any way, shape, or form like all the rest do. My experience with my four girls (and the multitudes of friends they have each had in their teen years) has taught me to expect the unexpected. My girls are similar in many ways, but they are unique as well. There are millions of factors that determine who they are becoming. And the differences have been beautiful to experience.

That being said, psychologists will tell you that puberty and the teen years for girls are often stormy and difficult. Dr. Michael Gurian (marriage and family counselor, pioneer of neurobiology and brain research, as well as a *New York Times* bestselling author of more than thirty books) stated, "Puberty is also perhaps the most frightening episode of life a girl experiences."[2] Why would this father of two girls and a heavily credentialed expert say this? Because stereotypes not only point to this type of experience but studies backed by research do as well. Well-known Christian counselor Sissy Goff, who recently shared this Gurian quote, went on to say:

> All girls go through some stage of narcissistic behavior. . . . They are going to be thinking about themselves a lot. . . . They are becoming their own people. . . . [It's] going to be really hard, and painful for them, and often painful for you too.[3]

Maybe you just grimaced a bit with that last statement, because lately you have watched as your girl struggles hard in her own skin. She who had the boldness at age nine to wear a princess dress to Walmart and charm her way into every friendship is now insecure, fussy, and has perfected door slamming to an art, which she does frequently as she hides in her room and refuses to engage with you. Or anyone other than her friends on BeReal. It is painful. Not only for you but for her as well.

I'm pretty sure every generation has dealt with this on some level. "There is," as Ecclesiastes 1:9 tells us, "nothing new under the sun." What has changed in the past fifteen years or so is the impact of social media and the rise of anxiety in girls (which we have already discussed). Plainly put, these days it might be harder to be a teen girl than it ever has before.[4]

During these (often) stormy teen years, I want to remind you of a couple of things I have realized over the past decade of raising my own teen girls.

First, parenting is a marathon. It is not a sprint. And, honestly, it doesn't end when you send them off to college or watch them walk down the aisle to marry their true love. You will parent for the rest of your life. Case in point, as I write this, my mom is boarding a plane to come and see me and my family for a few days. I am so happy about that. She will step through our front door and make everything wonderful. She will hug my girls and play board games with them. She will cook us dinner, and we will enjoy loving her well. I don't know what I would do without my mom these days, and I am well above my teenage years. I value her parenting possibly more today than ever.

Second, prayer is also a marathon. I can't really think of any serious heartfelt prayer I have only uttered once. Oh, sometimes my arrow prayers of *Lord, help!* or *I could really use a parking place* are one and done, but serious matters I've poured my heart out over to Jesus have sometimes taken years to see the fruit. These are forever prayers that I will probably pray for the rest of my life—or at least I'm willing to pray until the Lord gently places

His hand on my heart and says "Yes" or "No" for His glory and theirs and my good. Though the teen years last but a few seasons, your prayers will literally last for eternity (see Revelation 5:8). Parenting and prayer are long games, times forever. And even if the teen girl you are praying for is not your daughter, your prayers make her your spiritual daughter. My friend Robin is always quick to remind me, "The prayer of a righteous person is powerful and effective" (James 5:16). So, buckle up. Don't lose heart.

Wait, Can She Be Strong and Soft at the Same Time?

If you are working your way through this book chapter by chapter, you have likely spent the last week or so praying for your teen girl to be strong. You've probably turned on the news this week and thought, *Wow. This world is a mess. My girl will have to be strong in the Lord if she is going to survive.* You might even have grabbed your favorite worn-out Bible, placed it on the floor, and lain face down on it with tears streaming down your face. "Lord, make her strong" has become your fierce battle cry. And rightfully so. Please don't scratch that prayer off your list. It needs to remain consistently in your heart and on your lips.

So what do I mean by following up that seemingly bold prayer with a kinder and gentler prayer of "Lord, keep her soft"? Can she be strong and soft at the same time? I'm so glad you asked. As I was sketching out these prayers, I was so excited about these two chapters in the middle of this book. I see them as two sides of one coin. I was eager to share them with you because I think these two prayers are the very essence of what it means to be a girl in today's world, made in the image of God (the *imago Dei*), who is one-hundred-percent strong and one-hundred-percent soft at the same time. But before I show you that, let me tell you what I mean by soft. And to make it easy to remember, I've created an acronym. If you've read my other books, you know

I do love a good acronym because I have been known to forget my name on occasions, but not a good acronym.

S.O.F.T.

The *Merriam-Webster Dictionary* defines *soft* in various ways, including:

> pleasing or agreeable to the senses: bringing ease, comfort, or quiet; marked by a gentleness, kindness, or tenderness: such as *a* (1): not harsh or onerous in character . . . (2): based on negotiation, conciliation, or flexibility rather than on force, threats, or intransigence.[5]

You might use *soft* to positively describe your favorite cozy blanket or use it negatively to reflect a character you believe should be firm but has gone weak (for example, a judge we think should hold up a law but has gone soft due to popular opinion and influence). *Soft* can be a word chameleon for sure. But I want to lean into the part of the definition that says, "bringing ease, comfort . . . marked by a gentleness, kindness, or tenderness." Praying these characteristics over our teen girls will be like a breath of fresh air on the days we wonder if our words are merely hitting the ceiling. When I pray for my teen girl to be soft, I am asking God to do this in her life:

S—Help her to *see others.*

O—May she *offer an appropriate response* to what she encounters today.

F—Help her to believe that her *feelings are not a sign of weakness.*

T—Give her *time to quiet her heart* and truly rest from the onslaught of the day.

A soft teen girl will have to resist the sometimes-overwhelming biological urge to only focus on herself. She will have eyes that see others and realize that the teen years can be an amazing time to develop empathy and not demand it. But don't take my word for it. Science supports this possibility. Researchers Jessie Stern and Rachel Samson share this on the subject:

> In contrast to popular myths about self-obsessed teens, research shows that adolescence is a key stage of development for the growth of empathy: the ability to stand in someone else's shoes, to understand and resonate with their emotions, and to care about their well-being. Empathy is a skill that develops over time, and it has major consequences for teens' social interactions, friendships, and adult relationships.[6]

As your teen girl grows in empathy, she will be able to offer an appropriate response to her friend groups, the kids in the lunchroom at school, or in the comment section of her social media account.

At the same time, being soft will not encourage her to disregard her feelings but understand that she can feel them without embarrassment. Her feelings are part of who God is making her to be. They keep her real and relatable. In fact, when she can feel her feelings and process them with a safe adult, she herself will be a safe harbor for others according to Stern and Samson:

> Our research suggests that empathy starts with feeling safe and connected. Building secure relationships, characterized by trust, emotional safety, and responsiveness, can give teens a firsthand experience of empathy. With this foundation in place, they can then share that empathy with others.[7]

This type of softness takes time. Probably more time than we want to admit. But as we pray, may we be willing to help our teen girl recognize that she can't stay on the front line of the battle 24/7. She needs recovery time. She needs permission to rest, and yes, to do that in the privacy of her own room or quiet space where she can nap, craft, or dance if she wants to. She will also need a gentle reminder to study God's Word for herself, take time to pray, and journal.

A few weeks ago, one of my girls said to me, "Mom, I finally wrote in my journal today. I wrote six pages, and it really helped me process my thoughts and feelings. I don't know what took me so long to just do it." The truth is today's girls are busy. Like their moms, grandmas, and teachers. They have every space on their calendar filled with very important things. If you don't believe me, ask a twelfth-grade girl what she has on her plate today. And if she doesn't have an activity, she has filled in that space with worries she can't shelf. Her mind is busy even when her body isn't. The result is that we have a generation of girls who are hurting and get angry very quickly. Much of it could be mitigated if we gave them permission to not only feel their feelings but take the time to sort through them.

And yes, if you are wondering, I'm going to be praying these same exact prayers over my heart as well. How in the world can I ask God to do this in my teen girl's life when not five minutes ago I was raging at her in the car because she forgot to bring her math book to class? Friends, this chapter is equally messing with my own heart. But remember, I warned us of that in the beginning. We go first. But we don't have to go alone.

Jesus Is the Answer

If you are still wondering if it is possible to be both strong and soft at the same time, you don't need to look any further than Jesus. As both fully God and fully man, Jesus is our crystal clear example of how to be both.

- He was born quietly in a stable made for animals.
- He died an excruciating public and painful death that took incredible strength.
- He welcomed children to sit with Him.
- He cleared out the temple with righteous anger.
- He touched sinners.
- He defended the Word of God unapologetically.

Jesus wasn't mixed up. He was whole and complete. He was exactly what we needed—strong and soft. But what did Jesus say about Himself when given the opportunity? He said:

> Come to me, all you who are weary and burdened, and I will give you rest. Take my yoke upon you and learn from me, for I am gentle and humble in heart, and you will find rest for your souls. For my yoke is easy and my burden is light.
>
> Matthew 11:28–30

I love how author Dane Ortlund explains this passage:

> In the one place in the Bible where the Son of God pulls back the veil and lets us peer way down into the core of who he is, we are not told that he is "austere and demanding in heart." We are not told that he is "exalted and dignified in heart." We are not even told that he is "joyful and generous in heart." Letting Jesus set the terms, his surprising claim is that he is "gentle and lowly in heart."[8]

Jesus is strong enough to receive and carry all our burdens and soft enough to see us struggling under the weight of them. I don't know what the image of Jesus as "both and" does for your heart, but it fires me up and makes me want to cry simultaneously. I need Him desperately to be both strong and soft for me and my teen girls.

But here is a mind-blowing truth. Scripture tells us we are made in the image of God, and we can (and should) bear His strong and soft image to others as well. If you turn to Genesis, you will find these words:

> Then God said, "Let us make mankind in our *image*, in our *likeness*, so that they may rule over the fish in the sea and the birds in the sky, over the livestock and all the wild animals, and over all the creatures that move along the ground."
>
> So God created mankind in his own *image*,
>   in the *image* of God he created them;
>   male and female he created them.
>
> Genesis 1:26–27 (emphasis added)

I realize words originally written in another language can sometimes be hard for us to understand, especially when they get lost in translation. Recently, I found the nuance of the word *image* interesting. Maybe this will help with the point I'm trying to make. In her book *Everyday Theology*, Mary Wiley shares this quote from theologian Anthony A. Hoekema:

> In *Created in God's Image,* Anthony [A.] Hoekema discusses the Hebrew words for *image* and *likeness*, noting that *tselem* (image) is derived from "to carve," as a carved likeness of an animal or person, and *demuth* (likeness) indicates "an image which is like us." God chose to make us like Him in both form and image. You are both a picture of God and a representative of God on earth. That feels like a big responsibility, right?[9]

Of course, there are some ways we can't bear His image. We are not all knowing or all powerful. Clearly. But we can, through the power of His Holy Spirit, be strong in the strength of His might and represent His soft side by being kind, compassionate, and gentle as we carry His image to the world. It is a big responsibility. Jesus is the answer, and prayer is definitely the way.

Partnering with the Lord in prayer and asking Him to keep our teen girls soft is a lot like us handing the chisel and the hammer to the Lord and inviting Him to do the gritty work. We can't carve softness into their hearts on our own no matter how hard we try. That only comes from Jesus as He works on the rough edges, chiseling away the superfluous material that gets in the way of His softness coming in and through their lives. Remember, parenting and prayer are the long game, times forever. Give Jesus the chisel. Ask Him to do the work as the master sculptor.

"LORD, KEEP HER SOFT" PRAYERS

Romans 2:4—"Or do you show contempt for the riches of his kindness, forbearance and patience, not realizing that God's kindness is intended to lead you to repentance?"

> **PRAYER:** Father, thank you for your kindness toward _____ and that you wait patiently for her to turn from her sins. I pray that she will see your goodness as a gift that changes her old way of thinking and replaces it with your truth. In Jesus' name, Amen.

Matthew 11:29—"Take my yoke upon you and learn from me, for I am gentle and humble in heart, and you will find rest for your souls."

> **PRAYER:** Father, when _____ is tired and worn out, you invite her to come away with you to gently recover her life.

Your heart toward her is graciously kind. Show her how to take real rest, walk with you, and let you carry her burdens. In Jesus' name, Amen.

Galatians 5:22–23—"But the fruit of the Spirit is love, joy, peace, forbearance, kindness, goodness, faithfulness, gentleness and self-control. Against such things there is no law."

PRAYER: Father, the natural outworking of your Spirit is for _____ to look more like you. I pray that your Spirit will produce love, joy, peace, patience, kindness, goodness, faithfulness, gentleness, and self-control abundantly in her life. This is the result of your presence in her life so that others may see and know she is yours. In Jesus' name, Amen.

Colossians 3:12—"Therefore, as God's chosen people, holy and dearly loved, clothe yourselves with compassion, kindness, humility, gentleness and patience."

PRAYER: Father, I pray that _____ sees herself as chosen and well loved by you. May she dress herself spiritually with compassion, kindness, humility, gentleness, and patience as she gets ready for her day. In Jesus' name, Amen.

Ephesians 4:1–3—"As a prisoner for the Lord, then, I urge you to live a life worthy of the calling you have received. Be completely humble and gentle; be patient, bearing with one another in love. Make every effort to keep the unity of the Spirit through the bond of peace."

PRAYER: Father, may _____ live worthy of the high calling on her life. I pray she will have Christlike character and be filled with courage, integrity, humility, patience, gentleness, and love for others. May _____ do everything within her power to live as one and be at peace with those around her. In Jesus' name, Amen.

2 Corinthians 1:3–4—"Praise be to the God and Father of our Lord Jesus Christ, the Father of compassion and the God of all comfort, who comforts us in all our troubles, so that we can comfort those in any trouble with the comfort we ourselves receive from God."

PRAYER: Father, thank you that you are full of compassion toward us. When _____ is hurting, you offer deep comfort and encouragement to her. I pray that she will receive it and turn around and offer that same compassion, comfort, and encouragement to those in her life who are also hurting. In Jesus' name, Amen.

Galatians 6:9–10—"Let us not become weary in doing good, for at the proper time we will reap a harvest if we do not give up. Therefore, as we have opportunity, let us do good to all people, especially to those who belong to the family of believers."

PRAYER: Father, I pray that _____ will not grow discouraged in doing good, knowing that if she perseveres she will see the benefit someday. May she take every opportunity to always be helpful, especially to those who are closest to her—her sisters and brothers in the faith. In Jesus' name, Amen.

Matthew 5:7—"Blessed are the merciful, for they will be shown mercy."

PRAYER: Father, I pray that _____ will be blessed by the reciprocal nature of mercy. May she be sheltered by your promise that as she kindly cares for others, she will be kindly cared for by you. In Jesus' name, Amen.

Psalm 23:6—"Surely your goodness and love will follow me all the days of my life, and I will dwell in the house of the LORD forever."

PRAYER: Father, I love knowing that your goodness and mercy chase after _____ all the days of her life. Let her see clear evidence of that from the time she wakes up until she falls asleep, and may she be most at home in your presence. In Jesus' name, Amen.

Micah 6:8—"He has shown you, O mortal, what is good. And what does the LORD require of you? To act justly and to love mercy and to walk humbly with your God."

PRAYER: Father, you don't hide from _____ how you want her to live. I pray she will be fair, be kind to others, and not think too highly of herself. This is the good life you planned for her. May she walk in it always. In Jesus' name, Amen.

PRAYERS AND NOTES

7

LORD, SURROUND HER

Our God is fearless. And because *He* is fearless, we can be fearless too.[1]

Priscilla Shirer

I'm a beach girl. I love it all—the sun, sand, and sound of the waves crashing against the shore. Living in Florida does have its perks when you can jump in the car and be in your happy place in less than an hour. It doesn't happen nearly as often as I would like, but when it does, there is literally an unlocking of something in my soul that helps me breathe easier.

Now, even though I love the beach, I am not in favor of going in the water. I like looking at the water. I don't like being in the water. When my girls were little, my daughter Emma told her little sister Abigail, "I'm a waves girl. You are a sand girl." Me too, Abigail. Me too. I will walk the beach with you and look for seashells. I will bring a picnic lunch. And if the day is even more perfect, I will sit under the umbrella and watch all the beach bags, reading a book while you go in the water. I will not be riding those waves, sweet Emma. Of course, you know that.

Imagine my absolute horror when I saw an article online recently called "Watch Massive Sharks Swim Feet from Beach-goers in Florida."[2] The article said that on two separate occasions and two separate beaches, large sharks were seen in the shallow waters, weaving in and out of several groups of people who were having a leisurely day at the beach. If the words and pictures posted weren't enough, there are videos so you and I can watch this unfold as well.

Thankfully, no one was devoured by these close-to-beach-people sharks. They came and left. What surprised me was that even when people were running and shouting, "Shark! Get out of the water!" many of the people looked on without concern. They did not in fact leave the water. They stood there and took pictures.

No. Just no.

Friends, if I didn't keel over and die right there on the spot as those beasts were dodging in and out of swimmers, I would not have videoed this or posted on Facebook. I would have run for my life, grabbed my girls, and been in the car in two seconds flat. Beach day done. We are going home. And, even with my love for the beach, it would have been a good long while before I ventured back to the shore.

This is exactly what it feels like to pray for protection for my teen girls. It feels like we are having a lovely day on the beach, and danger suddenly appears and wreaks havoc in our lives. I want to run. I want to grab my girls and get out of there. But in the teen years, that is, for the most part, impossible. Think about it. Between the ages of twelve and twenty:

They go to middle school.

They go to camp.

They go to high school.

They learn to drive cars.

They leave in those same cars.

They go on dates.

They graduate from high school.

They get jobs.

They go away to college.

And not to be a drama queen, but those waters are teeming with all kinds of sharks. So what are we to do? How are we going to be okay with all this coming and going? Well, we could worry. We could let fear eat us from the inside out. We could hover like helicopters. We could choose to bubble wrap them forever and never let them go.

Or we could pray.

We could get on our knees and pray that God will go with them and give them peace that surpasses all understanding. We can pray for our hearts as well, as we smile, hug their necks, and wave from the front door.

We could pray, "*Lord, surround her.*"

When You Believe God More Than Anything Else

We like to think we live in the most precarious times. Maybe we do. Or, maybe we just have access to news 24/7 so we know more about the world we live in. When I study biblical history, I am always amazed at the courage it took for God's people to scrape out a life while enduring the constant threat of enemies. Or while living as slaves. One story of a woman in Scripture that has always captivated me is the story of Jochebed, the mother of Moses. You can find her story in Exodus chapter 2. She gets ten verses. That's all. But within those ten verses she does something that I would like to think I would have been able to do. I'd like to think I trust God like Jochebed did. But, if I'm being honest, I can't imagine it.

> Now a man of the tribe of Levi married a Levite woman, and she became pregnant and gave birth to a son. When she saw that he was a fine child, she hid him for three months. But when she could hide him no longer, she got a papyrus basket for him and coated it with tar and pitch. Then she placed the child in it and put it among the reeds along the bank of the Nile.
>
> Exodus 2:1–3

This story has context that starts in Exodus chapter 1. The new king of Egypt was worried about the Hebrew population. He ordered the midwives to kill all the boy babies. They quietly rebelled by not doing what he ordered and telling him it wasn't their fault. The Hebrew women were hardy. They birthed their babies before the midwives arrived. As a result, he made a new order: "Every Hebrew boy that is born you must throw into the Nile, but let every girl live" (Exodus 1:22).

Maybe Jochebed was one of those hardy Hebrew women. Maybe she was inspired by the Hebrew midwives. But when she became pregnant and saw her little guy, she did not kill him like the king demanded. She hid him until she couldn't hide him anymore. And then she got a basket, made it water resistant, and placed that basket in the Nile River with her fine child in it.

Jochebed put her beautiful baby boy in the same river where Pharaoh told the people to discard the babies. But she didn't just drop him in the river. She prepared a basket. She laid him in it. She gave him the best chance she could. Do I think she cried as she did it? Yes, I do. Do I believe she prayed as she worked and as she placed her son in the basket and launched him into crocodile-infested waters? Absolutely.

If you keep reading in Exodus, you probably know that Jochebed also sent Moses' sister to watch over him as he floated away from his mother. Moses ended up being delivered through the water to Pharaoh's daughter (how ironic!). She adopted Moses and even sent him back to Jochebed to nurse and care for him. This same Moses, raised by the royal family who originally wanted him and his Hebrew brothers dead, was used by God to deliver His people from 400 years of slavery.

How in the world was Jochebed able to do this? The book of Hebrews gives us the answer in one of the most popular passages in the Bible, commonly called "The Hall of Faith." It says, "By faith Moses' parents hid him for three months after he was born, because they saw he was no ordinary child, and they were not afraid of the king's edict" (Hebrews 11:23).

Jochebed (and her husband) had faith. They had the kind of faith that trusts in God more than anything else. More than logic would advise. More than circumstances would suggest. More than friends would recommend. She trusted in her God to take care of her child. No matter what. I want to trust God like that with my teen girl. Don't you? I know I can't actually put her in a tar-and-pitch papyrus basket and float her down the river, but I can prepare her. I can love her well in the process. And I can believe God more than my fears. You can too. We can both be like Jochebed because we can pray.

Praying in Real Time

Recently, our students volunteered during our church services as door greeters. They also helped pass out free T-shirts that say "For Orlando" to all of our church members. I love that my seventeen-year-old daughter is on the student serve team.

She literally comes alive when she has the chance to volunteer with her friends. After the service, I was waiting for her to finish up, and one of her friends walked up to her and said, "I want to invite you to go to Brazil with me next summer on a mission trip." As my daughter listened and asked calm and pointed questions, my brain ran fast toward the most imminent danger this trip could produce. Forget that it is sponsored by my mission-minded church. Forget that this sweet friend has been twice before on the same mission trip. Forget that her friend is also fluent in Portuguese. And forget that last year ten teenagers also went on the trip. Forget that this year several of my daughter's close friends might be going as well. This trip, looming in the future with so many unknowns, began to take me down a path that was going to be a quick, *No. You can't do that, and here are several reasons why not.* Until I realized that this trip could be amazing. It would be a great experience for her. She would love serving with her friends. It could build up her faith in extraordinary ways as well. Oh, and I also realized that she will be eighteen next summer. So, my grown-up girl will be old enough to decide if she wants to go to Brazil all on her own.

Honestly? I want her to go if God wants her to go. I want her to build up her bravery over the next few months, board a plane, and watch God work in ways she can't imagine in her life and the lives of those she meets in a faraway place. I did that in college, and it marked my life for good and showed me more of God's character than I could have learned otherwise. She can and should go if she wants to. But when and if that happens, I have to be ready to pray for her with the knowledge that I probably will not be able to go with her physically. That doesn't mean she goes alone. Not in the least.

Have you studied ancient Roman military strategies? No? Well, lucky for you and for me, my friend Erin knows about them. Erin is a Bible teacher and a mom of a teen girl. A few years ago, she shared with me about a defense tactic used by Roman armies called the *testudo* or Roman turtle formation. I've never forgotten it. And as a visual learner, this formation has become one of my favorite pictures of prayer. In the testudo formation, a group of soldiers would interlock their full-body shields on all sides of their huddle. The soldiers in the back would also take their shields and place them over the top of the soldiers like a turtle shell in order to cover them completely. Once fully protected, the group of soldiers would advance— together in a strong unit. Oftentimes, they would place injured soldiers or rescued people in the center of the formation because in the middle of this cohesive wall of shields there was safety.

When I pray for my teen girls, I visualize the testudo formation. I think about them being in the center of that safest place, and my prayers ask God to completely surround them. They are tucked in the testudo of God's protection. Psalm 91:4 (NLT) says it like this:

> He will cover you with his feathers.
> He will shelter you with his wings.
> His faithful promises are your armor and
> protection.

God's faithful promises are like a full body shield that defends and protects our girls (and us, for that matter). This place of safety is not only a strong, fortified fortress (think castle with an impenetrable defense), it is also a refuge from a sudden storm that they can run to at a moment's notice. It is here that our teen girls are kept. We likewise can pray, fully trust, and be at rest, knowing they might be swimming in a world teeming with sharks, but they are fully protected.

Where Is Your Faith?

I know this prayer falls in the category of easier said than done. I'm realizing that this is a theme in my life lately. So many things preach well, but they live hard. Sending our teen girls out the front door is not easy. But, the truth is, the world is coming for them inside our homes as well. We can't escape the fact that we aren't in control, and that is okay. Because we know who is in control.

That reminds me of one of my favorite stories about Jesus and His disciples in a boat headed to the "other side" of the lake (Mark 4:35–41 and Matthew 8:23–27). Settled in the boat with the waves hitting the side, Jesus goes to sleep, at which point all chaos breaks loose in the form of a relentless storm that has the boat covered in tumultuous waves. The disciples believe they are going to die and, terrified, cry out to Jesus to save them. Smart, that.

In Matthew's version, Jesus wakes up, and before He quiets the angry sea He asks the disciples a question. I happen to love *The Jesus Storybook Bible*'s version of this conversation: "Then Jesus turned to his wind-torn friends. 'Why were you scared?' he asked. 'Did you forget who I Am? Did you believe your fears, instead of me?'"[3]

When we pray for our teen girls and ask the Lord to surround them, we need to remember who Jesus is. We need to believe Him more than we believe our fears for them. Back to our friends in the boat with Jesus, here is how author Sally Lloyd-Jones finishes the story:

> Jesus' friends were quiet. As quiet as the wind and the waves. And into their hearts came a different kind of storm.
> "What kind of man is this?" they asked themselves anxiously. "Even the winds and the waves obey him!" they said, because

they didn't understand. They didn't realize yet that Jesus was the Son of God.

Jesus' friends had been so afraid, they had only seen the big waves. They had forgotten that, if Jesus was with them, they had nothing to be afraid of.

No matter how small their boat—or how big the storm.[4]

If you are finding it hard to pray "Lord, surround her," answer this question right now: *Have you forgotten who Jesus is?* It doesn't matter if your boat is the size of a tar-pitched papyrus basket or you are swimming with sharks on the beach. Jesus is with you, and He is with our teen girls. You have nothing to fear.

"LORD, SURROUND HER" PRAYERS

John 16:33—"I have told you these things, so that in me you may have peace. In this world you will have trouble. But take heart! I have overcome the world."

PRAYER: Father, you have told _____ in advance that she will experience trials and sorrows living in this world. But the good news is that in you she can have perfect peace and be filled with joy, knowing you have overcome it all. In Jesus' name, Amen.

Psalm 3:3—"But you, LORD, are a shield around me, my glory, the One who lifts my head high."

PRAYER: Father, you protect _____ on all sides. There is no place she is vulnerable to attack because you surround her. Be her glory. Lift up her head when she is weighed down by discouragement. In Jesus' name, Amen.

Psalm 71:3—"Be my rock of refuge, to which I can always go; give the command to save me, for you are my rock and my fortress."

> **PRAYER:** Father, I pray that you will be a stronghold that _____ will come to again and again because she feels safe within your care. In Jesus' name, Amen.

John 14:27—"Peace I leave with you; my peace I give you. I do not give to you as the world gives. Do not let your hearts be troubled and do not be afraid."

> **PRAYER:** Father, peace is your gift to _____ so that she doesn't have to be troubled or afraid. Your peace is not fragile like the world's version. Help her to know that it will be strong enough to see her through all the days of her life. In Jesus' name, Amen.

Psalm 91:4—"He will cover you with his feathers, and under his wings you will find refuge; his faithfulness will be your shield and rampart."

> **PRAYER:** Father, thank you that you protect _____ completely and that she can find shelter under your wings. I pray that your faithfulness will be the armor she chooses every day. In Jesus' name, Amen.

Psalm 23:4—"Even though I walk through the darkest valley, I will fear no evil, for you are with me; your rod and your staff, they comfort me."

> **PRAYER:** Father, if _____ finds herself walking through a dark valley, I ask that she will remember that you walk with her and she doesn't need to be afraid. I ask that you will bring

deep comfort to her during those times as you protect and guide her. In Jesus' name, Amen.

Zephaniah 3:17—"The LORD your God is with you, the Mighty Warrior who saves. He will take great delight in you; in his love he will no longer rebuke you, but will rejoice over you with singing."

> **PRAYER:** Father, because you are a mighty warrior who saves, _____ can have fearless confidence in you. May she hear the delight in your voice as you sing over her with a love song just for her. In Jesus' name, Amen.

Matthew 8:27—"The men were amazed and asked, 'What kind of man is this? Even the winds and the waves obey him!'"

> **PRAYER:** Father, I pray when _____ faces a life-threatening storm, she will remember that the winds and waves obey you and she can put her faith in you. In Jesus' name, Amen.

Ephesians 6:10–12—"Finally, be strong in the Lord and in his mighty power. Put on the full armor of God, so that you can take your stand against the devil's schemes. For our struggle is not against flesh and blood, but against the rulers, against the authorities, against the powers of this dark world and against the spiritual forces of evil in the heavenly realms."

> **PRAYER:** Father, I pray that _____ will draw her strength from you. May she put on your armor so she can stand safe against the tricks of the devil. Remind her that her enemies are not people but the spiritual forces of darkness. She doesn't need to be afraid, but she does need to be prepared. Your

armor is the perfect covering over her life, and she can choose it every day. In Jesus' name, Amen.

Hebrews 11:1—"Now faith is confidence in what we hope for and assurance about what we do not see."

PRAYER: Father, faith is the strong foundation that makes life worth living. Give _____ unshakable faith that keeps hoping even when she can't see the future. In Jesus' name, Amen.

PRAYERS AND NOTES

8

LORD, GIVE HER FRIENDS WHO ENDURE

A day without a friend is like a pot without a single drop of honey left inside.[1]

A. A. Milne, *Winnie-the-Pooh*

I heard her before I saw her. She had locked herself in the bathroom, and her tears were not the silent type. I stood on one side of the door, with her on the other, and thought to myself, *Will I make it worse or better?* I prayed a quick prayer and knocked softly. "Can I come in?" There was a significant pause before she slid the lock aside and opened the door with the tiniest bit of effort for me to squeeze through. It was only a crack. But it was all the invitation I needed.

I joined her on the floor and put my arms around her. "Do you want to talk about it?" Her crying increased before she handed me her phone for me to read hurtful words from someone who she thought was a friend. I'll confess I had to bite my lip not to join her in the crying session. I wanted to offer her support and perspective, but nothing breaks me like the tears of my girls. I also had a fair amount of mama-bear anger I had to push down as well, because how can teen girls be so mean? Still, after years of this scene replaying itself over and over in the lives of each of my four girls, I knew that my tears and anger would not serve her well at this moment. Instead, I sat with her until she dissolved into quiet hiccups of grief, and she told me what prompted the message (or so she thought). We processed together as I handed her tissues, got her a glass of water, and thought through her potential responses. We made a plan before she sweetly dismissed me and gathered her courage to turn the page and start fresh the next day.

If you asked my daughter if there was a single drop of honey-eyed friendship in the pot that day, she would probably tell you there certainly was not. If you asked any of her sisters, they would say, "Join the club. It was bound to happen at some point." Friendship and teen girls can be something of a minefield. Some days it is sweet; other days it explodes, and you are left to pick up the pieces. What might have simply been a truth in her early years ("She doesn't want to be my friend anymore") now becomes a label she wears that feels something akin to a scarlet letter ("I've been rejected and tossed aside by my best friend"). It can be debilitating.

Why is that? What changes in the teen years that elevates friendship to such a potentially destructive nature? Even after more than ten years navigating the teen years with my girls, and what feels like thousands of hours talking about how to develop healthy relationships during these years, I am no expert. But what I can tell you is that as storms come and go, friendships do as well. I have discovered that my girls can come through just about any situation when I am spending less time trying to fix it and more time on my knees, praying for her to first connect with the Lord and second be the friend herself she is so desperately seeking.

What a Teen Girl Wants

There seems to be a shift in the teen years for girls where they begin to define themselves by their relationships. Your teen girl is very aware of where she stands socially at school, church, clubs, or on her sports team. And as much as we have tried to debunk the ever-present stereotypes of teen girls and their narcissistic years, stereotypes also exist in her friendships. Girl squads. Mean girls. Bullies. Gossips. You can probably name them all. A teen girl's peer relationships can dethrone most (if not all) other relationships in her life. Her friends mean everything to her. At least in her eyes. And at the risk of this being a how-to book more than a prayer book, it would be helpful for us to think about what she needs and how we can pray her through these years.

What your teen girl wants more than anything is connection, to be known and valued. I remember wanting so badly to be connected to the girls in my school. Oh, they liked me well enough. But they hid large parts of their lives from me because I was more like the "mom" of the group. I clearly remember one Saturday night when a few friends told me they were going home and dropped me off at my house early. I found out later that they all went to a party. I was not invited and, quite frankly, probably wouldn't have gone anyway. My biggest fear came true when the connection I thought was real snapped and they didn't want me tagging along. I felt entirely disconnected. Maybe this is why:

> Friendship is a reciprocal relationship characterized by intimacy, faithfulness, trust, unmotivated kindness, and service. The concept can describe one's relationship with people and with God.[2]

What my sixteen-year-old heart longed for was trust and reciprocity. In that instance I realized they were missing. Our teen girls feel the same way. They are looking for the type of relationship that says, "I'm your friend just like you are my friend." The trouble with this hardwired need and her developing emotional intelligence in the teen years is that she (and her peers) may not be very good at true reciprocity or even know how to choose friends who can provide it for them as well. Reading social cues and understanding how to keep good boundaries can be a challenge for our teen girls. When they were little girls, they had playdates with an adult nearby to settle disputes and give much-needed breaks with milk and chocolate chip cookies. As teens they tend to gather just outside of our peripheral vision within growing friend groups. We are mostly finding out about their relationships (good or bad) after the fact.

Don't get me wrong, friendships in their teen years can be beautiful and heartfelt. I've watched my teen girls take a leap of faith, reach out, connect with a new friend, and see God bless them in the most extraordinary way. I've watched as sweet friends text my' girls, send Bible verses, and offer support when life has gone sideways. That deep need for connection can and does work well at times. I've never been more grateful than when my girls have a safe place to cultivate friendships that draw them closer to who God is creating them to be.

For example, in the middle of writing this chapter on teen girls and friendships, I left my cozy coffee shop, stopped by the store, and picked up the ingredients for pumpkin muffins. My daughter was invited to a picnic and wanted to share them with the girls who would be attending. This group is made up of both senior girls and freshman girls from our church. My daughter's friend (also a senior) wanted to do something special for the younger girls because when she was that age, the older girls in her former church were unkind to her and her friends. She not only set up the picnic but also encouraged and challenged the other senior girls to step into a mentoring relationship. My daughter was hooked instantly.

Several freshman girls came, and sweet connections were made. I love that these senior girls recognized that even when friendships hurt, you can choose to dwell in that pain or give it to God and change the story. I couldn't help but think that this type of friendship born out of hurt fits so well with these verses:

> Praise be to the God and Father of our Lord Jesus Christ, the Father of compassion and the God of all comfort, who comforts us in all our troubles, so that we can comfort those in any trouble with the comfort we ourselves receive from God. For just as we share abundantly in the sufferings of Christ, so also our comfort abounds through Christ.
>
> 2 Corinthians 1:3–5

I can't wait to see what develops in the next few months after phone numbers were traded over those pumpkin muffins and plans for a Christmas party were discussed. The comfort of Christ changes the story for everyone and is beautiful to see, especially in the lives of our teen girls.

What a Teen Girl Needs

While your favorite teen girl is looking for friends in her peer group, we know what she really needs is a deeply satisfying relationship with Christ. Jesus is perfect at the type of closeness she craves. Hebrews 13:5 tells us that Jesus will not walk away from us. He certainly won't uninvite us from being His friend via direct message. He stays. Always. Still, who can blame her for wanting a friend who is there right now to grab Starbucks with and swap stories of a hectic day at school? We want that for her too. Author Christine Hoover in *Messy Beautiful Friendship* said it like this:

> . . . we tend to make people our gods. We look to them—at least I have—to know us intimately at all times, to meet our every need, to be there when we want them near, and to love us unconditionally and perfectly, when the map points only to God as having these abilities.[3]

Guess what? I want that for my own heart. The challenge comes when we focus entirely on the person and miss that they can't really be everything we need. As we pray for a teen girl, we need to be bold enough to pray that her first friendship will be Jesus. That she will define her life by His unconditional love for her, model her life after His, and look for friends who point her to Him every step of the way.

I've mentioned my friend Brooke already, but you might not know that she has written a similar book called *Praying for Teen Boys.* If you have a teen boy in your life, you need it too. Our books are complementary but have some differences between them, as you can expect. One way our books are the same is that we realize having friends who get our teens to Jesus is powerful. Brooke (who has two teenage boys) reminded me of a story in Scripture that epitomizes the type of relationships we want our teens to have—no matter if they are girls or boys. You can find it in Mark 2:1–4:

> A few days later, when Jesus again entered Capernaum, the people heard that he had come home. They gathered in such large numbers that there was no room left, not even outside the door, and he preached the word to them. Some men came, bringing to him a paralyzed man, carried by four of them. Since

they could not get him to Jesus because of the crowd, they made an opening in the roof above Jesus by digging through it and then lowered the mat the man was lying on.

Jesus drew a crowd wherever He went, and often getting within hearing distance was a challenge. I love that someone offered up their home as a makeshift pulpit for Jesus to preach the Word. In this case, so many people pushed in to hear Him, the doorway was blocked. Meanwhile, there were a few friends in the crowd who had one mission in mind—they wanted to get their paralyzed buddy to Jesus. He couldn't take himself, and they couldn't afford to wait. So what were the four friends to do? These friends made a way where there didn't seem to be one. They tore the roof off the place to lower and position their friend right in front of Jesus. His response was classic: "When Jesus saw their faith, he said to the paralyzed man, 'Son, your sins are forgiven'" (Mark 2:5). Their boldness moved Jesus to heal their friend, first of his sins and then of his ailment (see verses 10–12). Everyone who was watching was amazed and said, "We have never seen anything like this!" (Mark 2:12).

A passage like this stirs something in me. I want to have that kind of bold faith to put my teen girl at the feet of Jesus. But at the same time, I want her to have friends who will do that as well. Of course, I'm going to take her needs and requests to Him. But what will happen to her heart when her closest friends have faith when hers is wounded? What about the days she can't find a way to get herself to sit at His feet and pray? What if her faith is weak after days and months of praying and seeking Jesus? Can friends who not only point her to Jesus but will carry her to Him with such determination make a difference? Is that the richest type of honey in the pot of friendship? Yes and amen.

Here's the Thing about Social Media

No matter how we might wish it weren't a thing, social media is here to stay. I will tell you, though all my girls have begged to be on social media, they have also willingly (and not so willingly) removed themselves from all forms of it at times. It is a crazy dance between wanting to be part of it and sometimes understanding the dangers that lurk under the surface of likes, comments, and selfies. I think girls are especially at risk in the area of making and keeping friends in a social media world. Social media (and smartphones in general) remove the personal and face-to-face interaction we need to develop healthy friendships. Consider this as well:

> Peer acceptance is a big thing for adolescents, and many of them care about their image as much as a politician running for office, and to them it can feel as serious. Add to that the fact that kids today are getting actual polling data on how much people like them or their appearance via things like "likes." It's enough to turn anyone's head. Who wouldn't want to make themselves look cooler if they could? So kids can spend hours pruning their online identities, trying to project an idealized image.[4]

That idealized image can be hard to maintain too. This is nothing new for teens—especially teen girls. We all wanted to be liked and have friends when we were their age. What has changed is that social media magnifies everything. It can create false identities, provide spaces for bullies to show up, and give us a strong sense of FOMO—fear of missing out. Who hasn't seen a social gathering we were not invited to and wondered, *Why was I left out?* The party I mentioned when I was sixteen would have certainly had pictures online today, and I would have seen it with my own eyes before I heard about it in the hallway Monday morning at school. Seeing would have been worse. Funny how social media can create strong feelings of loneliness when it doesn't acknowledge the fact that we all feel loneliness at some point in our lives.

The point is that teen girls are growing up in a new generation where much of life is lived in online spaces. My friend Mary Margaret West is an expert in ministry to girls, and she says:

> Girls growing up now are digital natives and have had technology as part of their entire lives. I've watched some toddlers who can navigate an iPad easier than their parents. The girls in our churches, communities, and lives are online more often than they are in-person. Have you watched a group of girls sitting in the same room sending texts or Snapchats to each other? It's easy for a lot of us adults to say we don't have time to be where they are online, or that we don't want to be on another platform, but we could be missing opportunities to see what's going on in the lives of girls if we're absent . . . we don't want to fuel gossip or point fingers but the door is often wide open to start conversation. Social media isn't all bad, and we would be wise to be where girls are.[5]

Guess what? We are also digital natives—as parents, grandparents, and mentors. We are walking with our teen girls through this online world for the first time too. Our experience is happening simultaneously. But what is different is we have a fair amount of life lived without it being something we needed to manage. Can I make a suggestion? Don't just judge your girl's social media consumption and warn her of the negative effects of it in her life. I mean, for sure encourage boundaries for her and talk about how often she is online, but also follow your teen girl on social media. Use it to start conversations and as a prayer prompt for her. Especially in the area of her friendships. As you look at images of her and her girlfriends, pray for each of those sweet smiles. Pray they will know Jesus, live for Him, and cheer each other on to love and live for Him as well.

What about Dating?

I know you might have expected me to say more about dating in this book, because here we are in the last couple of chapters, and I haven't mentioned it at all. The teen years are, after all, filled with opportunities for outrageous prom proposals (when did that become a thing?), hangouts, and coffee dates. It may be in these years that your girl develops her first crush and experiences firsthand what heartbreak feels like. And though I could devote an entire book to this subject, I simply want to take this approach: Dating is a form of friendship, and the prayers I offer here apply as well. I want my teen girl's first love to be Jesus. I want it to fill her up and define her life. I want her to have good boyfriends who are kind and faithful. I want my teen girls to be in dating relationships (when they are ready) that are marked by trust and reciprocity. And I absolutely want her boyfriend to be willing to get her to the feet of Jesus when she is struggling. I want her to be that kind of friend to him as well.

I realize there are deeper issues that may come up, like honoring God with their physical relationship and how much time is wise to spend exclusively dating when they might (and probably will) go separate ways during the college years. I do not want to downplay those issues at all. I just think if we are actively praying through all the other prayer themes in this book, this one will fall into line as well. However, if you are still finding yourself a bit concerned about this area in your teen girl's life and worried about the boys who are texting and asking her out for dates, I'd love to offer you this perspective from Bible teacher Jen Wilkin based on Song of Solomon 8:8–9, which says, "What shall we do for our sister on the day she is spoken for? *If she is a wall*, we will build towers of silver on her" (emphasis mine). I think it supports what I've been saying all along:

> Instead of intimidating all your daughter's potential suitors, raise a daughter who intimidates them just fine on her own. Because you know what's intimidating? Strength and dignity. Deep faith. Self-assuredness. Wisdom. Kindness. Humility. Industriousness. Those are the bricks that build the wall that withstands the advances of Slouchy-Pants, whether you ever show up with your Winchester locked and loaded or not. The unsuitable suitor finds nothing more terrifying than a woman who knows her worth to God and to her family.[6]

Pray she will be strong and soft.
Pray she will have deep faith.
Pray she will be wise and kind.
Pray she knows her worth to God and her family.
Pray she will be a wall and that God will bring a boyfriend into her life who realizes she is worth knowing.
Because she absolutely is.

"LORD, GIVE HER FRIENDS WHO ENDURE" PRAYERS

John 15:13—"Greater love has no one than this: to lay down one's life for one's friends."

> **PRAYER:** Father, you showed us how to be a true friend by laying down your life for us. I pray _____ will be a friend like Jesus. May she put her life on the line for her friends and point them back to you. In Jesus' name, Amen.

1 Corinthians 13:4–7—"Love is patient, love is kind. It does not envy, it does not boast, it is not proud. It does not dishonor others, it is not self-seeking, it is not easily angered, it

keeps no record of wrongs. Love does not delight in evil but rejoices with the truth. It always protects, always trusts, always hopes, always perseveres."

PRAYER: Father, I pray that _____ will experience your real, life-changing love today. May she see the patience, kindness, trust, and hope in your enduring love and let it flow through her to others. In Jesus' name, Amen.

Proverbs 17:17—"A friend loves at all times, and a brother is born for a time of adversity."

PRAYER: Father, give _____ the kind of friends who love her no matter what. I pray she will have friends who feel more like family and stick with her during difficult times. In Jesus' name, Amen.

Proverbs 27:17—"As iron sharpens iron, so one person sharpens another."

PRAYER: Father, a good friend will help _____ be better in every way. I pray she will have friends who encourage and challenge her and that she can do the same thing for them. In Jesus' name, Amen.

Ruth 1:16–17—"But Ruth replied, 'Don't urge me to leave you or to turn back from you. Where you go I will go, and where you stay I will stay. Your people will be my people and your God my God. Where you die I will die, and there I will be buried. May the LORD deal with me, be it ever so severely, if even death separates you and me.'"

PRAYER: Father, a loyal friend is hard to find. I pray that you will help _____ be the kind of friend who doesn't walk away from others in their time of need. Give her faithful friends for all of her life. In Jesus' name, Amen.

Hebrews 10:24–25—"Let us consider how we may spur one another on toward love and good deeds, not giving up meeting together, as some are in the habit of doing, but encouraging one another—and all the more as you see the Day approaching."

PRAYER: Father, I pray that _____ will be a true encouragement to her friends and do everything she can to help them grow in their faith. Give her loving, kind, and supportive friends who build her up and don't tear her down. In Jesus' name, Amen.

Mark 2:3–4—"Some men came, bringing to him a paralyzed man, carried by four of them. Since they could not get him to Jesus because of the crowd, they made an opening in the roof above Jesus by digging through it and then lowered the mat the man was lying on."

PRAYER: Father, give _____ devoted friends who will pray for her and take her to you when she can't get there herself. I pray the faith of her friends will move her to believe in you more. In Jesus' name, Amen.

Romans 12:10—"Be devoted to one another in love. Honor one another above yourselves."

PRAYER: Father, let _____ be a part of a group of friends who have authentic affection for one another. May they love one another deeply and put the needs of each other above their own. In Jesus' name, Amen.

1 Thessalonians 5:11—"Therefore encourage one another and build each other up, just as in fact you are doing."

PRAYER: Father, I pray that _____ will build others up with hope. May they in turn strengthen her faith and cheer her on as she lives for you. In this type of friendship there is no competition but mutual support. I pray you would give _____ friends like that. In Jesus' name, Amen.

Ecclesiastes 4:9–10—"Two are better than one, because they have a good return for their labor: If either of them falls down, one can help the other up. But pity anyone who falls and has no one to help them up."

PRAYER: Father, you tell us that two are better than one because we are made for community. Please give _____ at least one good, true-hearted friend who believes in you and will help her get up when she falls down. In Jesus' name, Amen.

PRAYERS AND NOTES

9

LORD, LIGHT HER PATH

If only the next step is clear, then the one thing to do is take it. Don't pledge your Lord or yourself to any steps beyond what you know.[1]

Amy Carmichael

I'd like to think she had good intentions. Her timing wasn't really all that spectacular, although considering the timeline, maybe she felt her opportunity to speak with Jesus was now or never. I will say this for her—she was bold enough to ask.

> Then the mother of Zebedee's sons came to Jesus with her sons and, kneeling down, asked a favor of him.
> "What is it you want?" he asked.
> She said, "Grant that one of these two sons of mine may sit at your right and the other at your left in your kingdom."
> "You don't know what you are asking," Jesus said to them. "Can you drink the cup I am going to drink?"
> "We can," they answered.

Jesus said to them, "You will indeed drink from my cup, but to sit at my right or left is not for me to grant. These places belong to those for whom they have been prepared by my Father."

Matthew 20:20–23

Jesus was on His way up to Jerusalem with His small entourage of followers. As they were walking, He took the time to pull His disciples aside to tell them what was going to happen. He was going to be arrested, be condemned, die, and rise from the dead. I don't get the feeling this was a lighthearted discourse. I think Jesus was providing a passionate, heartfelt commentary on what was going to test them all to the core.

To her credit, Mama Zebedee approached Jesus with respect. She asked to make a request. Her posture (like the mother from Matthew 15) was worshipful. By all appearances she was honoring Jesus and His position. He responded by simply asking her, "What do you want?" Given the green light to ask for a favor, she stated it plain as day: *I want my boys to rule with you and beside you. I want them to have places of authority too.*

I think as she made her request, Jesus saw through it as actually being a request made by James and John. And so, He answered her sons (not her directly) with a statement and a question. He told them they didn't know what they were asking and said, "Are you able to drink the cup of suffering I will drink? You know, the one I just told you about?" Their confidence would be cute if it wasn't so cocky. Jesus knew they would be asked to follow in His footsteps, but right then, they had no idea what was ahead. He then added that their request was really up to the Father to decide.

Do you know what I see in this story? I see a mom who clearly loved Jesus and her kids. She wanted the best for them.

I wonder, though, if days later, standing at the foot of the cross with Jesus' own mother, if she thought about what He said to her and her boys that day on the road: *You don't know what you are asking.* I wonder if she wanted to take it back. I don't blame her if she did. Knowing the road her sons would take in the days that followed, I tend to think her own heart was tested to the core as well.

The Question Gets Harder to Answer

One simple question total strangers felt free to ask my girls was "What do you want to be when you grow up?" The fact that these were the same people who told me how hard it was to raise girls doesn't bother me at all. Well, at least not much. It is a common question kids get. I find it funny that at six years old my girls knew exactly what they wanted to be—a cupcake shop owner, a fashion designer, or a professional mermaid (I'm assured they do exist). By the time they graduated from high school, my girls, like so many others, hesitated when asked that same question. Where did that confidence go that was one-hundred-percent sure she wanted to be a Disney princess? Where is that girl today?

Recently I organized a very unofficial survey for teen girls regarding prayer. I thought as I was writing this book it might be a good idea to ask a few teen girls what they thought about prayer and what they wanted most from those who prayed for them. I shared with them the theme of each chapter and asked, "In what area do you need prayer most?" Overwhelmingly, respondents said, "I need prayer to find my purpose." It was nearly double the next two categories of prayer for friends and prayer to feel loved and pursued by God. But what else captured my attention was this: 64 percent of the girls who took the survey agreed with the statement "I need all the prayer I can get." I hope that encourages you to pray today. This prayer journey is not for the faint of heart. Keep in mind, it is probable that your teen girl might respond differently if you ask her these same questions from the survey. It is easier at times to answer questions from a stranger than from your mom, mentor, or grandmother. One girl told me in the comment section:

> I wish the previous question was a "Select All That Apply" because I definitely feel that I need prayer to be strong and protected from outside, extraneous circumstances that constantly weigh me down and burn me out.

Do you know what that tells me? Our teen girls want to be prayed for every single day. They want you to be bold enough to ask Jesus for a favor on their behalf. They want to believe prayer works. Wouldn't it be amazing if they saw us position ourselves before Jesus and ask these requests on their behalf? I think that girlish confidence might grow to look more like a mature faith that fitted them for their future in a way that we can't possibly predict. Our teen girls might one day be asked to dream big dreams and take brave steps that point others to Jesus. Or they might be asked to follow Jesus on a hard path filled with suffering. And though we might pray for the first and against the latter, more than anything we want to pray, "Lord, light her path" so that she will take the next right step no matter what.

Being versus Doing

It is entirely possible that we've been asking the wrong question when it comes to purpose. We tend to focus on what we should do more than who we should be. And as we think through praying for teen girls, it is wise to remember they are still in the process of becoming, developing, and changing. Can we really expect a teen girl who is still figuring out who God has made her to be to know what to do with all that potential? I've always loved how Ephesians 2:10 frames this process: "For we are God's handiwork, created in Christ Jesus to do good works, which God prepared in advance for us to do."

When I look at this verse, I see three key points as we think about our teen girls:

1. Your girl is the work of God's hands. The original Greek language here uses the word *poiēma* for handiwork, which is obviously where we get the word *poem* from in the English language. Your teen girl is like poems written by God. She has depth, color, emotion, and truth written in, over, and through her. God is speaking through her beautiful life, and it is something only He can say. Your teen girl is a masterpiece.

2. Your girl is created in Christ Jesus and invited to join Him in the work He is doing. When she comes to faith in Christ, she gets a personal invite to work with Jesus. In fact, the evidence of His saving grace is His good works displayed in her life. What is the work Jesus is doing? Jesus said He came to seek and save the lost (Luke 19:10), to give us abundant life (John 10:10), and to glorify His Father (John 17). The beautiful part about this is that she does not do this work in a vacuum or alone. As she walks with Christ in daily life, she participates in His work.

3. God has already planned the good works your girl gets to do. There really isn't a guessing game here. Before

she was born, God knew and planned those good works she was going to be part of, and here is the most beautiful truth: She isn't performing for God—He is divinely working through her.

Part of how all this works is that your girl has unique gifts and talents given to her by God to use on His behalf to do these same good works. Interestingly enough, according to Barna research, teens are "eager to know and grow their gifts":

Across the board, younger respondents have bigger and more emphatic responses to the topic of gifting. This could reflect their generational ambition and passion as well as their youth as they navigate new seasons of personal and occupational development.[2]

As a group, teens are not only aware of their gifts but are also working toward becoming better in their use of them. My teenage daughter, for example, took an entire class devoted to helping her be strong and mindful of how God wired her. She is well-versed in StrengthsFinder, Myers–Briggs, and her core values. She knows her love language and her best learning style. Even with all this self-knowledge, she asks bigger questions about what she should be doing with her life. I'm trying to move her toward the conversation of her being who God made her to be, to walk with Him faithfully, and to trust Him with what comes next.

Slow and Steady Wins the Next Right Step

You are probably familiar with Aesop's fable "The Tortoise and the Hare." It is a cute story about two competitors who approach their race differently. The tale has a moral we can recite by memory: Slow and steady wins the race. My girls always loved this fable because the winner isn't who you'd expect. I recently heard a real-life story about two groups of explorers who were on a journey to the South Pole in 1911. One group chose to travel only when the weather was favorable. On those days they went hard and fast for about forty to sixty miles. The other group made a commitment to march twenty miles each day, no matter what. They traveled a little bit every day without fail. Guess which group made it to the South Pole first? The group who day-in-and-day-out took the next right step. As it turned out, the other group not only lost, they all died.[3] I find it intriguing that even difficult circumstances, which often throw us off course, were not an excuse to miss taking one (even small) step toward their desired outcome.

I recently read a book by author Emily P. Freeman called *The Next Right Thing.* In her opening chapter on the topic of figuring out your purpose in life, Emily states,

> Regardless of your own degree of personal choice, you have a God who walks and talks with you, who moves in and through you, who sings over you. How he moves in you may be different from how he moves in me, but one thing is certain. He remains unchanged. As my friend and teacher James Bryan Smith so kindly reminds us, you are one in whom Christ delights and dwells, and you live in the strong and unshakable kingdom of God. The decision is rarely the point. The point is you becoming more fully yourself in the presence of God.[4]

When I look back on my life, I can see how the decisions I made about where I went to college and how I spent my time impacted who I would marry and where I would one day live and work. But the most important part of those years, filled with big, life-changing decisions, was understanding my relationship with God. When something big came up and I didn't know what to do, I sought the Lord. When the way was not clear, I paused. On the other hand, if I knew where He was leading me and fear tried to paralyze me, I asked Him to light my path clearly. Do you know what He did? He showed me the way. It wasn't always the way I wanted to go or that I felt made the most sense, but not once did God ever leave me alone in the process. And because I knew Him better each day, I was able to follow His lead.

Can you imagine your teen girl truly understanding that God delights in and dwells with her? What would she be able to say *yes* to if she believed herself to be part of that strong and unshakable kingdom of God? Who would she be if the point wasn't the decision that needed to be made but was about becoming her wholehearted self in His presence? I think she would become that living masterpiece He has always intended her to be. And it would truly be a work of art.

How God Lights Her Path

Several years ago, when we moved to Florida, one of the things I noticed was that there was an abundance of light every single day. I've grown accustomed to it after all these years. So much so that when we have a rare rainy day in the Sunshine State, I feel it deep within my soul. It's funny—growing up in the Midwest, I didn't realize what I was missing. It wasn't that there wasn't light at all; it was just dimmed for many days. I crave the light now. I also see the way light is a key theme throughout Scripture. From Genesis to Revelation, God has used light to pierce the darkness, cause things to grow, and show us the way.

In Psalm 119, the writer makes this connection with light and the Word of God: "Your word is a lamp for my feet, a light on my path" (Psalm 119:105). This is such a great visual for our "next right step" because the lamp isn't a large beacon. It is small and handheld, giving just enough light for you to put one foot in front of the other. His Word also illuminates the path, so we know what direction we are heading. We don't have to be afraid of the dark or the next step. God has lit the way with His Word.

I love that passage, but there is more about light that I want to share with you as you think about praying for your teen girl. It might even bring you a measure of peace in your own life. You see, in the book of John we read:

> In the beginning was the Word, and the Word was with God, and the Word was God. He was with God in the beginning. Through him all things were made; without him nothing was made that has been made. In him was life, and that life was the light of all mankind. The light shines in the darkness, and the darkness has not overcome it.
>
> John 1:1–5

John beautifully describes Jesus as both the light and the Word. He is the Word made flesh who came to dwell among us. He is the Light of the World who overcame darkness through His life, death, and resurrection.

Jesus talked about light too when He said, "I am the world's Light. No one who follows me stumbles around in the darkness. I provide plenty of light to live in" (John 8:12 MSG). Our teen girls need to be able to see from the perspective of God, who knows all and sees all. I want my girls to always remember that in Christ they have plenty of light to live in. Jesus is the light of the world and the Word made flesh, which means that where He dwells there is light and hope. He came to show them (and us) the way. And the world can't overcome it. Not for a moment.

A Leap of Faith

So, where does this leave us as we pray that the Lord will light her path? Well, I think we approach the Lord with the right attitude and ask Him for the things that matter most. I think we go ahead and ask for big things and let Him say yes, no, or not yet. I also believe we need to encourage our teen girl to grow in her giftedness and affirm her when we see it. And, when she is tempted to focus too much on the gifts, we can remind her that it is God who is working through her one beautiful life, and she doesn't need to work for Him to gain that approval. I think we also need to be mindful to watch and pray when she is facing big decisions. I think it also helps to bring her favorite snack while she is studying for her big math test and whisper in her ear, "God is walking with you through this, and He will light the way for you just enough to show you the next step."

I shared previously in my book *Being OK with Where You Are* about one of my favorite movie scenes, and it applies here as well. I can't think of a better visual for this important prayer for our teen girls.

In the 1989 movie *Indiana Jones and the Last Crusade*, Indy (played by Harrison Ford) had to take a leap of faith. Running for his life (of course), he came to a giant precipice and was faced with a decision. He needed to get to the other side, but there was no obvious path. Would he find a way to keep going? Would he turn back? Could he take the next step? With his heart pounding, he suddenly remembered the words "leap of faith." He took a fortifying breath, lifted his foot, and placed it down on thin air. But when his foot fell, it was touching solid ground. Suddenly, the leap of faith turned into a bridge of faith. His human eyes could not see it. The bridge was only accessible by faith.[5]

Sweet friend, the path your teen girl is walking is best seen with the eyes of faith. She is somewhere in the process right now of deciding if she will choose to trust or turn back. Honestly, the next step may feel like she is stepping on thin air. What can you do? You can go to your knees and cover her with these prayers. And while you are praying, ask God to remind her that He has gone before her and installed a bridge of faith. She simply must have faith to be able to see it.

"LORD, LIGHT HER PATH" PRAYERS

Psalm 119:105—"Your word is a lamp for my feet, a light on my path."

> **PRAYER:** Father, you don't leave _____ in the dark but you give her your Word so that she can see where to take the next step. Keep the pathway lit so she doesn't stumble or fall. In Jesus' name, Amen.

Jeremiah 29:11—"'For I know the plans I have for you,' declares the LORD, 'plans to prosper you and not to harm you, plans to give you hope and a future.'"

> **PRAYER:** Father, your plan for _____, even in hard times, is to take care of her and not leave her alone. I pray she will grasp the good thoughts and hopeful future you have for her and believe you for it. In Jesus' name, Amen.

Romans 8:28—"And we know that in all things God works for the good of those who love him, who have been called according to his purpose."

PRAYER: Father, I pray that _____ will have sweet confidence that you work all things for her good and your glory. As she loves you and seeks your purpose for her life, remind her of this truth. In Jesus' name, Amen.

2 Timothy 1:9—"He has saved us and called us to a holy life—not because of anything we have done but because of his own purpose and grace. This grace was given us in Christ Jesus before the beginning of time."

PRAYER: Father, you have rescued _____ and called her to a holy way of life. May she realize that it isn't because of what she has done to deserve salvation, but it is a result of your undeserved grace. I pray this alone will set her free to know she doesn't need to earn it. It's been hers from the beginning and granted to her through Christ. In Jesus' name, Amen.

Psalm 86:12—"I will praise you, Lord my God, with all my heart; I will glorify your name forever."

PRAYER: Father, may _____ give thanks to you with her whole heart and honor your name always. In Jesus' name, Amen.

James 4:13–15—"Now listen, you who say, 'Today or tomorrow we will go to this or that city, spend a year there, carry on business and make money.' Why, you do not even know what will happen tomorrow. What is your life? You are a mist that appears for a little while and then vanishes. Instead, you ought to say, 'If it is the Lord's will, we will live and do this or that.'"

PRAYER: Father, I pray that _____ will live her life seeking and trusting your will more than her plans. Show her your path and plan so she can follow you wholeheartedly. In Jesus' name, Amen.

Isaiah 25:1—"LORD, you are my God; I will exalt you and praise your name, for in perfect faithfulness you have done wonderful things, things planned long ago."

PRAYER: Father, when _____ looks back I pray she will see all the amazing things you have done in the past and how perfectly faithful you have been to your children. Let this give her hope that you will be the same today and tomorrow as you were yesterday. In Jesus' name, Amen.

2 Corinthians 5:7—"For we live by faith, not by sight."

PRAYER: Father, I pray that _____ will live by what she believes, not by what she can see merely with her eyes. Give her faith to build a bridge if that's what is needed. In Jesus' name, Amen.

Deuteronomy 31:8—"The LORD himself goes before you and will be with you; he will never leave you nor forsake you. Do not be afraid; do not be discouraged."

PRAYER: Father, you go before _____ and you are always with her. I pray she will not be fearful or worried about what lies ahead but take courage, knowing you will not fail her in this or anything else. In Jesus' name, Amen.

Romans 15:4—"For everything that was written in the past was written to teach us, so that through the endurance taught in the Scriptures and the encouragement they provide we might have hope."

PRAYER: Father, thank you for giving _____ your Word—filled with truth and stories that show us what to do and how to keep our hopes up. Let your Word be a deep encouragement to her heart when she has questions or is not sure of your will. I pray she will return to it again and again. In Jesus' name, Amen.

PRAYERS AND NOTES

ACKNOWLEDGMENTS

After doing this nine times now, I can say without hesitation that books are never the work of the writer alone. It is a total team effort from beginning to end. I'm fortunate to have the best people who are for me and these words in the most amazing way:

Mike, Emma, Abigail, Caroline, and Alison: Thank you for being so supportive and for encouraging me every step of the way. You have prayed, read rough drafts, listened as I processed, and cheered me on when I needed it most. It is not easy living with a writer. Thank you for loving me well!

Mom: Thank you for praying for me every day of my life and pointing me to Jesus. If I am half the prayer warrior you are, mountains will move. I love you so much.

Tanya Cramer: Your support and work on this project mean more than I can say. Thank you for reading every word, correcting my wayward grammar, and telling me the truth I needed to hear when I wanted to quit. You are literally the best.

Edie, Erin, Amy, and Angie: Jesus was so kind to bring you into my life. Thank you for listening to me wrestle over this book and for praying me through to the very last page. LYLAS.

Robin: Your faithful prayers have availed much. Thank you.

Haley: Working with you has been a sweet blessing. Thank you for helping me to adjust to my new role at First Orlando and for allowing me the margin to write these words. I could not have done this without you.

Brooke: I have learned so much from your heart for prayer! Thank you for believing in me and this project. I'm honored to be side-by-side with you once again! We really do bring out the best in each other!

Kate: Thank you for adding your words to this book. I'm so glad that one day long ago you left a comment on a blog post and that as a result we became friends in real life. I am grateful for you!

Jeff: I feel like this is a full circle moment that started with hope over a decade ago. I am excited to finally be working with you and the entire Bethany House team. Thank you for making this project the best it can be!

Janet and the Books and Such Agency: Thank you for working relentlessly to make this project a success! Let's keep going!

Jesus: Thank you for making this reluctant prayer warrior believe. Help my unbelief.

RECOMMENDED RESOURCES

Prayer Resources:
Praying for Boys by Brooke McGlothlin
Praying for Teen Boys by Brooke McGlothlin
Praying for Girls by Teri Lynne Underwood
Praying Mom by Brooke McGlothlin
Prayer by Timothy Keller
Fervent by Priscilla Shirer

Recommended Books Previously Mentioned:
Humility by Andrew Murray
Get Out of Your Head by Jennie Allen
Don't Miss Out by Jeannie Cunnion
Everyday Theology by Mary Wiley
The Next Right Thing by Emily P. Freeman
Gentle and Lowly by Dane Ortlund
Messy Beautiful Friendship by Christine Hoover
Show Her the Way by Mary Margaret West
You Are My Hiding Place by Amy Carmichael

Uninvited by Lysa TerKeurst

Keep a Quiet Heart by Elisabeth Elliot

The Jesus Storybook Bible by Sally Lloyd-Jones

None Like Him by Jen Wilkin

NOTES

Chapter 1 Lord, Show Me How to Walk in Humility

1. Andrew Murray, *Humility: The Beauty of Holiness* (Abbotsford, WI: Aneko Press, 2016), 52.

2. Leon Morris, *The Gospel according to Matthew*, The Pillar New Testament Commentary (Grand Rapids, MI: W.B. Eerdmans, 1992), 405.

3. Brooke McGlothlin, *Praying Mom: Making Prayer the First and Best Response to Motherhood* (Minneapolis: Bethany House Publishers, 2021).

4. Jennie Allen, *Get Out of Your Head: Stopping the Spiral of Toxic Thoughts* (Colorado Springs: WaterBrook Publishers, 2020), 162.

5. Erika Allen, *ESV Prayer Journal: 30 Days on Humility* (Wheaton, IL: Crossway, 2022), definition page.

Chapter 2 Lord, I Believe. Help My Unbelief.

1. Timothy Keller, *Prayer: Experiencing Awe and Intimacy with God* (New York: Penguin Books, 2016), 24.

2. Annie F. Downs, "Let's Read the Gospels," AnnieFDowns.com, November 1, 2023, https://www.anniefdowns.com/letsreadthegospels/.

3. *Strong's Definitions*, Blue Letter Bible, s.v. "G342. anakainōsis," accessed August 12, 2023, https://www.blueletterbible.org/lexicon/g342/kjv/tr/0-1/.

Chapter 3 Lord, Pursue Her Heart

1. Lysa TerKeurst, *Uninvited: Living Loved When You Feel Less Than, Left Out, and Lonely* (Nashville: Nelson Books, 2016), 30.

2. "U.S. Teen Girls Experiencing Increased Sadness and Violence," CDC. gov, February 13, 2023, https://www.cdc.gov/media/releases/2023/p0213-yrbs.html.

3. Anita Slomski, "Teen Girls Are Faring Worse Than Boys on Nearly All Mental Health Measures—Here's Why," *JAMA Medical News* 329, no. 15 (March 2023): 1243–45, https://jamanetwork.com/journals/jama/article-abstract/2803138.

4. *The Chronicles of Narnia: Voyage of the Dawn Treader*, directed by Michael Apted, (20th Century Studios and Metro-Goldwyn-Mayer, 2010), DVD.

5. Kevin W. Larsen, "El Roi," *The Lexham Bible Dictionary*, ed. John D. Barry et al. (Bellingham, WA: Lexham Press, 2016), accessed on Logos Bible Software.

6. "Beer-Lahai-Roi," *The Lexham Bible Dictionary*, ed. John D. Barry et al. (Bellingham, WA: Lexham Press, 2016), accessed on Logos Bible Software.

7. Francis Thompson, "The Hound of Heaven," 1850, http://www.houndofheaven.com/poem.

Chapter 4 Lord, May She Seek What Is True

1. Mary Wiley, *Everyday Theology: What You Believe Matters* (Nashville, TN: Lifeway Press, 2019), 14.

2. Joe Carter, "9 Things You Should Know About Prayer in the Bible," The Gospel Coalition, U.S. Edition, May 7, 2015, https://www.thegospelcoalition.org/article/9-things-you-should-know-about-prayer-in-the-bible1/.

3. Carter, "9 Things You Should Know About Prayer in the Bible."

4. Noah Webster, *An American Dictionary of the English Language*, s.v. "sanctify," https://webstersdictionary1828.com/Dictionary/sanctify.

Chapter 5 Lord, Make Her Strong

1. Elisabeth Elliot, *Keep a Quiet Heart* (Ann Arbor: Servant Publications, 1995), 106.

2. *Merriam-Webster*, s.v. "empower (v.)," accessed September 23, 2023, https://www.merriam-webster.com/dictionary/empower.

3. Jeannie Cunnion, *Don't Miss Out: Daring to Believe Life is Better with the Holy Spirit* (Minneapolis: Bethany House Publishers, 2021), 109.

4. Kenneth L. Barker, *Micah, Nahum, Habakkuk, Zephaniah*, vol. 20, The New American Commentary (Nashville: Broadman & Holman Publishers, 1999), 377.

5. Blue Letter Bible, s.v. "strength," accessed September 23, 2023, https://www.blueletterbible.org/lexicon/h2428/kjv/wlc/0-1/.

Chapter 6 Lord, Keep Her Soft

1. Jen Wilkin, *None Like Him: 10 Ways God Is Different from Us (and Why That's a Good Thing)* (Wheaton, IL: Crossway, 2016), 38.

2. Michael Gurian, *The Wonder of Girls: Understanding the Hidden Nature of Our Daughters* (New York: Pocket Books, 2002), 38.

3. Sissy Goff, "Psychologist Michael Gurian calls these years," Instagram video, July 3, 2023, https://www.instagram.com/p/CuQLtJPAXhL/.

4. Sissy Goff, "Psychologist Michael Gurian calls these years," Instagram video, July 3, 2023, https://www.instagram.com/p/CuQLtJPAXhL/.

5. *Merriam-Webster*, s.v. "soft," accessed October 9, 2023, https://www.merriam-webster.com/dictionary/soft.

6. Jessie Stern, Ph.D. and Rachel Samson, M.Psych, "How to Build Teens' Empathy," August 3, 2021, *Psychology Today*, https://www.psychologytoday.com/us/blog/the-heart-and-science-attachment/202108/how-build-teens-empathy.

7. Stern and Samson, "How to Build Teens' Empathy."

8. Dane Ortlund, *Gentle and Lowly: The Heart of Christ for Sinners and Sufferers* (Wheaton, IL: Crossway, 2020), 18.

9. Mary Wiley, *Everyday Theology: What You Believe Matters* (Nashville: Lifeway Press, 2019), 115–16.

Chapter 7 Lord, Surround Her

1. Priscilla Shirer, *Fervent: A Woman's Battle Plan for Serious, Specific, and Strategic Prayer* (Brentwood, TN: B&H Books, 2015), 113.

2. Sage Marshall, "Watch Massive Sharks Swim Feet from Beachgoers in Florida," *Field & Stream*, July 7, 2023, https://www.fieldandstream.com/survival/shark-sightings-florida-beaches/.

3. Sally Lloyd-Jones, *The Jesus Storybook Bible* (Grand Rapids, MI: Zondervan, 2007), 242.

4. Sally Lloyd-Jones, *The Jesus Storybook Bible* (Grand Rapids, MI: Zondervan, 2007), 242.

Chapter 8 Lord, Give Her Friends Who Endure

1. "50 Cute Best Friend Quotes about True Friendship," SouthernLiving.com, June 2, 2013, https://www.southernliving.com/culture/best-friend-quotes.

2. Justin Langford, "Friendship," ed. Douglas Mangum et al., *Lexham Theological Wordbook*, Lexham Bible Reference Series (Bellingham, WA: Lexham Press, 2014), accessed on Logos Bible Software.

3. Christine Hoover, *Messy Beautiful Friendship: Finding and Nurturing Deep and Lasting Relationships* (Grand Rapids, MI: Baker Books, 2017), 37–38.

4. Rachel Ehmke, "How Using Social Media Affects Teenagers," Childmind.org, updated May 2, 2024, https://childmind.org/article/how-using-social-media-affects-teenagers/.

5. Mary Margaret West, *Show Her the Way: Your Guide to Discipling Teen Girls* (Nashville, TN: Lifeway Press, 2019), 25.

6. Jen Wilkin, "On Daughters and Dating: How to Intimidate Suitors," The Gospel Coalition, U.S. Edition, June 23, 2014, https://www.thegospelcoalition.org/article/on-daughters-and-dating-how-to-intimidate-suitors/.

Chapter 9 Lord, Light Her Path

1. Amy Carmichael, *You Are My Hiding Place* (Bloomington, MN: Bethany House Publishers, 1991), 25.

2. Barna Group, "Gen Z Are Leaning Into Their Gifts: Will the Church Help?", Barna.com, January 5, 2022, https://www.barna.com/research/gen-z-gifts/.

3. Todd Zipper, "The 20-Mile March: Are You Amundsen or Scott?", Medium.com, March 23, 2016, https://medium.com/monday-motivator/the-20-mile-march-are-you-amundsen-or-scott-144e404087e2.

4. Emily P. Freeman, *The Next Right Thing: A Simple, Soulful Practice for Making Life Decisions* (Grand Rapids, MI: Revell, 2019), 16, Kindle: Loc 206.

5. *Indiana Jones and the Last Crusade*, directed by Steven Spielberg (Hollywood, CA: Paramount Pictures, 1989).

STACEY THACKER is a speaker and the author of nine books, including *Hope for the Weary Mom* and *Threadbare Prayer: Prayers for Hearts That Feel Hidden, Hurt, or Hopeless.* She has a passion to encourage women in their walks with God and currently serves as the director of women's ministry at First Orlando. Stacey and her husband, Mike, live in Central Florida with their four daughters. You can find her online at StaceyThacker.com or on Instagram @staceythacker.

You May Also Like . . .

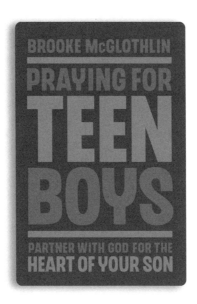

Helping you navigate the complicated teen years—and your changing relationship—with your son, Brooke McGlothlin offers wisdom, practical help, and over 90 Scripture-inspired prayers to help you fight for your teen, not against him. Feel purposeful, not powerless, in your parenting as you partner with God in prayer—and rediscover the joy of being his mom.

Praying for Teen Boys

PRAYERS AND NOTES

PRAYERS AND NOTES

PRAYERS AND NOTES

PRAYERS AND NOTES

PRAYERS AND NOTES

PRAYERS AND NOTES

PRAYERS AND NOTES

PRAYERS AND NOTES

PRAYERS AND NOTES